P9-DWX-934

TWO TRUTHS AND A LIE

Brought to you by your local library with funding
from the Idaho STEM Action Center.

IDAHO
STEM
ACTION CENTER

ICfL Idaho
Commission
for Libraries

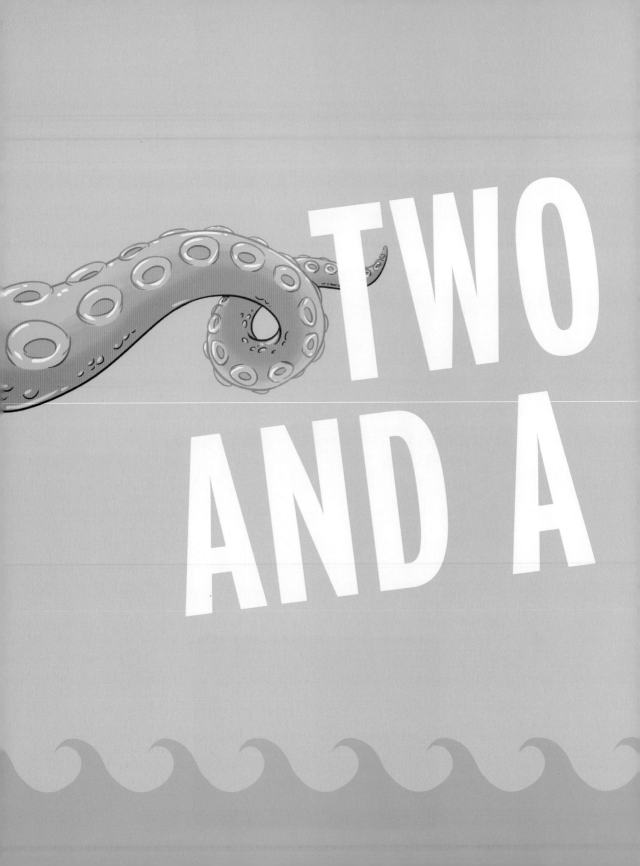

TRUTHS

LIE

It's Alive!

AMMI-JOAN PAQUETTE
and LAURIE ANN THOMPSON

WALDEN POND PRESS
An Imprint of HarperCollinsPublishers

Walden Pond Press is an imprint of HarperCollins Publishers.

Walden Pond Press and the skipping stone logo are trademarks and registered trademarks of Walden Media, LLC.

Two Truths and a Lie: It's Alive!

Text copyright © 2017 by Ammi-Joan Paquette and Laurie Ann Thompson
Illustrations copyright © 2017 Lisa K. Weber
All rights reserved. Printed in the United States of America.
No part of this book may be used or reproduced in any manner whatsoever without written permission except in the case of brief quotations embodied in critical articles and reviews. For information address HarperCollins Children's Books, a division of HarperCollins Publishers, 195 Broadway, New York, NY 10007.
www.harpercollinschildrens.com

Library of Congress Control Number: 2016950349
ISBN 978-0-06-241879-1 (trade bdg.) — ISBN 978-0-06-241881-4 (pbk.)

Typography by Aurora Parlagreco
18 19 20 PC/WOR 10 9 8 7 6 5 4 3 2

❖

First Edition

For all those who love a good story but
aren't afraid to seek the truth

CONTENTS

INTRODUCTION

You should know something right up front: this book is sneaky.

Everybody knows the way books normally work. If you pick up a work of fiction, you know that most of what you will read in between those covers is made up. It's a delicious creation straight from the imagination of the author. If you pick up a nonfiction book, then you can count on the contents being true and factual. But this book is not all fiction nor all nonfiction. Instead, it's a bit of both.

See? Sneaky.

All around us, everywhere in the world, there are lies. But there are truths, too. And sorting out one from the other is a really important—and seriously interesting—part of life.

So here's the way this book works. Each section is broken down into chapters and each chapter consists of three stories. If you've read the book's title, I bet you know where we're going with this. In every single chapter:

- **Two** of the stories are 100%, cross-your-heart-and-hope-to-die TRUTHS

- and **one** of the stories is a complete fabrication—a LIE!

But which is which? Ah, that's where *you* come in. Even the lies might have kernels of buried truth. And some of the truths are so unbelievable, they will scramble your brain! Your mission is to separate the two.

So pull up a chair and settle in for a rocking good read. Just remember: don't take these stories at face value. Read them. Talk them over with your friends. Do your own research. Dig around online (safely, of course!). When it comes to information—and life, really—asking good questions is a kind of superpower.

And the answers are out there, we promise.

They're just waiting for you to find them.

PART 1

PREPOSTEROUS PLANTS AND FUNGI— CRAZY, CREEPY, COOL

Ah, nature. A green meadow. Wind rustling through the leaves. Mushrooms growing on the side of a fallen log. What could be more peaceful, more predictable, more ordinary?

To that we say: ha! The plants and fungi we spotlight in this section are full of surprises. They completely defy those common stereotypes and misconceptions!

Intrigued? We hope so! Because once you've read these, *going green* will never again mean quite the same thing. . . .

A. UNDERGROUND MIRACLE ROOT

Picture this scene: You're a farmer living in rural China, and you're out digging up medicinal herbs and roots. Most of the roots you find are skinny and stringy and wispy. But today's discovery is nothing like that. The plant that's buried deep in the moist ground in front of you is rounded and heavy. You unearth your prize, which is bigger than both your hands put together, and to your delight you see that this root is . . . person-shaped?!

Can you believe this grew under the ground?

Congratulations! You've just dug up a royal fleeceflower root, known locally as *he shou wu* or *fo ti*. Mainly found in rural areas of northeastern China, this rare and highly prized root is an offshoot of the common tuber

fleeceflower, a medicinal herb that's used for liver and kidney health, for better blood circulation, to remove toxins from the body, and more. This uncommon strain, the royal fleeceflower, has similar healing properties but in concentrated form: extra strong, in other words.

But what makes it *really* special? It's shaped like a little person. Specifically, the royal fleeceflower root is distinctive for its limb-like growths that oddly mirror the human form.

Hard to believe? Maybe not. Royal fleeceflower is found in particularly soft yet rocky soil: instead of growing into the flat, bulbous shape of the standard fleeceflower root, its royal cousin pushes around obstructions in its way, giving the fully matured root its rounded, uniquely doll-like appearance.

While royal fleeceflowers are farmed for medicinal use, a growing number of horticultural exporters are eyeing the roots *not* for grinding, boiling, and extracting of healing properties, but rather for decoration. After all, who *wouldn't* want a little root-goblin brightening up the coffee table. Er . . . right?

Do you see the resemblance?

Now, you should know that not *every* royal root dug up is going to look like your great-aunt Susan. "The truth is, maybe one in four royal fleeceflowers have any human resemblance at all," says Dr. Chen Jie, associate professor of horticulture at Oregon State University, who has published several well-regarded papers on the plant. "Most are closer to a lumpy ginger root." But ever since photos of a royal fleeceflower root with an apparent resemblance to Homer Simpson went viral in 2013, plant lovers worldwide have been falling over themselves to get their hands on the prized tubers. That's not as easy as it might seem. The USDA's Animal and Plant Health Inspection Service classified it as a restricted import in 2014, to the great frustration of exporters and collectors alike.

So for the foreseeable future, at least, the royal fleeceflower will have to go on being admired from afar. Unless you happen to have access to just the right moist patch of earth: by a stream, perhaps, where a certain shoot will spark a burst of excitement. You pull out your gardening trowel and start to dig. . . .

Plants: Fact or Fake?

All of these are scientifically true, except for one! Can you figure out the fake?

1. Bananas are not simple fruits. They are berries.

2. Cucumbers are not vegetables. They are fruits.

3. Peanuts are not nuts. They are legumes.

4. A sunflower is not one flower. It is a cluster of tiny florets.

5. Carrots were not originally orange. They were purple.

6. Vanilla flavoring comes from the seedpod of an orchid.

7. Spinach is not a vegetable. It is a fungus.

8. Cashews are not nuts. They are drupes that grow on the ends of cashew apples.

9. Strawberries aren't berries. They are accessory fruits.

10. Peaches, pears, apricots, and apples are all members of the rose family.

B. PANDOMONIUM

Imagine a forest. Now imagine that forest covering more land area than 100 football fields. Next, imagine that the entire forest is actually just one very large, very heavy, and very old tree!

This spectacular tree, called Pando, is very real, and you can visit it in the Fishlake National Forest in Utah. On the surface, Pando looks like a typical forest of quaking aspen, with up to 47,000 individual trees visible. But looks can be deceiving.

Below the ground, scientists now know that all of those trees sprouted from the same connected root system—in other words, the whole forest is really one massive tree—making it one of the largest living things on Earth. The total weight of all the parts of this extraordinary plant is approximately 13 *million* pounds! That makes Pando the heaviest known single organism, too.

Perhaps even more surprising is the fact that every one of those trees is an identical clone of one original tree that spawned them all long, long ago. While that specific tree is no longer alive, its genetic code is in every single tree that makes up the Pando organism today.

Pando, which means "I spread" in Latin, has been spreading from that original tree for a long time. No one knows for sure exactly when Pando started growing, but scientists estimate it was at least 80,000 years ago. Some say it could even be up to a million years old. That would make Pando not only one of the largest and heaviest living things on Earth, but also one of the oldest—it could have started growing before modern human beings even existed!

Since it can repeatedly clone itself and spawn new saplings, Pando has enjoyed a kind of

Logan
Brigham City
Ogden
Layton
Bountiful
Salt Lake City
West Valley City
Sandy
Orem
Provo
Duchesne
Nephi
Price
Delta
Castle Dale
Fillmore
Richfield
Hanksville
Torrey
Beaver
Junction
Cedar City

Wyoming

Utah

Fishlake National Forest

immortality since it first sprouted. And, because it can extract nutrients from the ground anywhere in its root system and ferry them along to wherever they're most needed across the entire clone network, Pando can survive many negative environmental conditions that would wipe out other kinds of trees.

So, will Pando just keep spreading forever? Unfortunately, experts fear it may now be in danger. Like other quaking aspen groves throughout North America, Pando is suffering from something called "sudden aspen decline" or SAD. Caused by extreme drought and high temperatures, SAD may leave affected trees weakened and more vulnerable to bugs, fungi, and animals—and it may even kill them. SAD and other factors are causing

Cloned trees growing from a single aspen root

Pando to do something it has never really done before: age. The older trees that make up Pando are doing fine, but the younger shoots are no longer thriving. There are not enough new clones joining the older ones, so the average age of the trees in the Pando forest is rising quickly.

Botanists: scientists who study plants

But some people are trying to help. **Botanists** are studying SAD to better understand its causes and effects. Others are clearing small stands of older trees in hopes of encouraging new stems to sprout, and they're putting up fences there to keep deer and elk from eating Pando's tender young shoots. Will these efforts be enough? Only time will tell. But, hopefully, time won't run out for Pando.

Try This!

1. Invent your own original plant. How tall is it? Does it bear flowers or fruit? If so, what do they look like? What conditions does the plant need to thrive? Draw a color diagram and summarize its most interesting qualities. Then, make a sculpture of your creation using pipe cleaners and colored tissue paper.

2. Start a nature journal. Sketch interesting leaves or flowers you find in green spaces near you. Keep a record of what you find and where you found it. Don't forget to include your personal observations, such as what your discoveries look like, how they smell, what they feel like, and more.

C. THE SECRET LIVES OF PLANTS

You may think that plants just sit there, soaking up the sun and growing ever so slowly. But there's a lot going on inside those roots and stems that you probably aren't even aware of. Get ready for a fascinating sneak peek at the inner life of plants!

First: Plants can sense things that are important to them, like light, water, and nutrients. And they can react, too. Plants can move to seek out sunlight or grow more roots where soil is better. And of course there are plants like the Venus flytrap, which snaps shut when an unsuspecting fly tickles the hairs on its leaves. (Dinner!)

Second: Would you believe that plants can learn? Botanists have shown that the more times a plant responds successfully to a particular sensation, the better it will respond the next time. Practice makes perfect, apparently even for plants! That's a pretty impressive feat for organisms that don't even have brains, don't you think?

Third: As crazy as it sounds, plants can communicate! When an antelope nibbles on an acacia tree, for example, that tree will start to produce a **toxin** that makes its leaves bad tasting and harder to digest. The tree also emits a gas as a warning signal to other acacias! Up to fifty yards away, acacia trees will receive the message and

WARNING: Dine at your own risk!

start producing more toxin in their leaves, too. So watch out, antelope . . . the trees are joining forces to ruin your midday meal!

Toxin: a poisonous substance made by a living organism

"Mom was right. It IS a great day to sprout!"

Plants can also communicate with their not-yet-sprouted seeds. Mother plants can pass on information that tells their seeds how soon to sprout based on recent weather conditions. Studies have also shown that plants are somehow able to pass on what they've learned to future generations, including ways to survive extreme heat, resist infections, and combat animals that try to eat them. As usual, mama knows best, even if you're a plant.

Plants even have ways of communicating with other species!

Take Action

Find a plant identification book or website for your region (ask an adult if you need help), and learn to identify some of the plants in your neighborhood. Then take someone with you on a walkabout to show them what you've learned!

Flowers tend to be colorful and smell a certain way to attract the right kinds of birds and insects to pollinate them. And many plants use thorns or toxins to warn herbivores—animals who eat plants—to stay away. But it gets a whole lot weirder than that!

One study showed that trees in a forest can use fungi growing between their roots to tell one another important news about what's happening throughout the forest, such as a drought or insect attack. The trees can also use this fungus "network," sometimes referred to as the wood-wide web, to deliver water and other nutrients from trees that are thriving to trees that are in need. It's almost like they've constructed a fungus telephone system, complete with 911 emergency services.

And, speaking of calling 911, some plants can even rally an animal army to come to their defense! When caterpillars attack plants like corn or lima beans, for example, the plants send out a chemical distress signal. The scent then gets picked up by wasps, which race in to attack the caterpillars. The plants are saved, and the wasps get a tasty caterpillar dinner. It's nice to have friends you can call on in a pinch!

Plants may not have brains and nervous systems like we do, but they can still do some pretty amazing things in their own special ways: sensing and reacting, learning, and communicating with one another and with entirely different kinds of organisms. They probably have a lot to tell us, too . . . if we're willing to listen.

SO, YOU'VE JUST READ *about the weirdly shaped royal fleeceflower from China; the vast interconnected forest-which-is-also-one-giant-tree called Pando; and a roundup of super plant tricks, including their ability to communicate with one another and even with different species! All three of these stories are hard to believe—but two of them are actually true. Can you figure out which one is not?*

A. THE FLOWERY SMELL OF DEATH

Let's talk about flowers. People love flowers! They're so bright and beautiful. They have colorful petals. They smell sweet. All of those things are true . . . *usually*. But wouldn't you know it? You're about to meet a flower that breaks just about every one of those rules.

Introducing: the *Amorphophallus titanum*. Or, among friends, the corpse flower.

Yes, you read that right.

It's a flower that sort of looks and very much smells like day-old roadkill.

The corpse flower is native to the Indonesian island of Sumatra and was first cataloged by Italian botanist Odoardo Beccari in 1878. Calling it a flower isn't entirely accurate, though. The *Amorphophallus titanum* is actually an inflorescence—a cluster of flowers grouped together on a single plant. It has a tall stalk called a spadix with a cluster of tiny flowers along the base, covered by a crimson skirt called a spathe. The gigantic plant can weigh over 100 pounds, and it can easily outgrow a basketball player. The tallest recorded corpse flower was over 10 feet high!

But the corpse flower's real claim to fame? It *stinks*.

Not always, mind you. In fact, not even very often. The corpse flower spends most of its time underground, with just one big leaf out, as the plant stores up energy for the big show to come. It can stay this way for up to 10 years, never blooming once. Then one day, the corpse flower begins to shoot up, growing as much as six inches per day. Finally, it's show time: the flower begins to open. The

Hold your nose and duck for cover: It's the corpse flower in bloom!

top of the spadix turns into a mini heater, getting up to 10 degrees warmer than the surrounding air—as warm as a human body, in fact.

And that's when the smell kicks in. Pee-yew!

If only this were a scratch 'n' sniff book, you could get the full experience. Instead, you'll have to imagine it for yourself: Take one part stinky gym socks, one part rotten fish, one part poopy diaper. Add a dash of raw garlic and strong Limburger cheese, and ooze in a sickly sweet crushed-flower smell.

A dab of that fragrance on your neck, perhaps? No?

Well, believe it or not, there *is* a good reason for this stomach-churning aroma. "Instead of being pollinated by bees, the corpse flower is pollinated by flies," says Suzanne Lijek, a biology teacher at Belmont High School, in Belmont, Massachusetts. The insects fly into the flower, get all covered in pollen, then fly away. Lijek brought a smaller breed of corpse flower into her classroom in 2012. "My students could smell it from way outside the classroom. After a while, though, you get used to it."

The flower only grows wild in the rainforests of Sumatra, but it has been successfully cultivated all over the world. Many

institutions that grow the stinky plant have come up with creative names for their blooms, including "Morticia" at the Franklin Park Zoo in Boston, "Putrella" at the Muttart Conservatory in Edmonton, "Spike" at the Chicago Botanic Garden, and "Edgar Allan Pew" at the Volunteer Park Conservatory in Seattle.

This putrid pollinator has certainly found its way to stand out. Somewhere around the world—maybe in a greenhouse or a public garden near you—a corpse flower is beginning its slow cycle of growth. It might be years before the bloom sees the light, but when it does . . . oh, boy. Everyone around will know it.

And in the end, what could be sweeter than that?

Talk It Out

From the tiniest mustard seeds to the tallest giant sequoia trees, plants are amazing! They're extremely diverse and very different from us, and we're completely dependent on them for our survival. Imagine you're a plant scientist. What kinds of plants would you most like to study? What questions do you have about how plants live? What problems exist in the world today that might be solved by learning more about plants? What aspects of the plant world do you find the most fascinating? Why?

B. EYES WATCHING FROM THE DARKNESS

The woods are quiet. So quiet you could hear a cricket cough or a sunbeam smile. But there are no sunbeams *this* deep in the woods. And the farther you walk—hopefully you're not by yourself—the more you start to feel like there's *something* out here with you.

If you've ever felt the prickly sensation of unseen eyes staring at you in the dark, dark forest, you might have had an unknowing encounter with the slyrking. Is it a bug? Is it a plant? It's neither. Not exactly, anyway; this moss is a **hybrid** of the two. The slyrking, more commonly known as walking moss, was first identified on the frozen tundras of the Santharia region of Svalbard, an **archipelago** off the coast of Norway.

Svalbard, home of the walking moss

To the casual eye, the slyrking looks much like any other ordinary patch of moss: a furry carpet of dense, close-growing dark-green tufts. And, if you're observing it in the light of day, that's likely all you'll see. But just wait until the frozen darkness falls; what you see then might surprise you. The walking moss, well, walks. Or "creeps" is perhaps a better way to describe it: its movement is so slow it's nearly impossible to see without time-lapse photography— barely six inches per hour.

An individual slyrking measures between two and three inches long, and its underside is covered with flagella—tiny lash-like "legs" that propel it along the ground. But slyrking are rarely seen alone; instead, they link together in packs of several dozen—and sometimes up to

Beware the lurking slyrking!

Hybrid: two different species mixed together

Archipelago: a scattered group of islands

four or five hundred. "It's a form of camouflage," says Eleanna Kalrinwenens, research assistant at Reading University in the United Kingdom. "Slyrking have evolved to take on the appearance of their surroundings. When they're stationary, they're nearly indistinguishable from common mosses."

Slyrking are heterotrophs, a type of organism that gets its nutrients from organic sources. What does this mean for our intrepid eaters? In the quiet of the night, the slyrking creep along in search of a decomposing animal. When they find one, the creatures move to cover up the corpse. Then, the feasting begins! The slyrking remain in place until the bones are picked clean and every last nutrient is extracted. Mmmm-mmm. These food elements can be stored for weeks, months, or even years: however long it takes for the slyrking to come upon their next meal.

First encounters with slyrking were recorded in the late 1960s, when Svalbard's shrinking glaciers uncovered huge areas of land that were formerly permafrost. Permafrost is ground that has been frozen for at least two years, but the area around Santharia might have been in deep freeze for upward of a century. "The thaw seems to have brought the walking moss out of a long-term hibernation," says Kalrinwenens, who joined members of the Norwegian Polar Institute in analysis and identification of this new species. Since then, walking moss has been recorded in the icy forests and tundras of Alaska, northern Canada, Siberia, and

Real Plant Names (Mostly)

All but one of them are real. Which one do you think isn't?

1. Sneezewort
2. Dinosaur food
3. Venomous tentacula
4. Butter-and-eggs
5. Devil's walkingstick
6. Kangaroo paw
7. Mother-in-law's pincushion
8. Monkey puzzle tree
9. Kiss me over the garden gate
10. Stinking Christopher

Greenland.

So next time you're out for a frosty picnic, be careful where you spread that blanket. That patch of moss you're sitting on might be more alive than you expect—and hungrier!

A FUNGUS AMONG US

A **parasitic** fungus that takes over the minds of its hosts and forces them to do its bidding? It sounds like something straight out of a horror movie. Believe it or not, it happens on multiple continents every single day!

Several species of the fungus *Ophiocordyceps* (off-ee-oh-COR-duh-seps) are well known for just this sort of behavior. The fungus infests hosts—usually ants—when the insects accidentally eat some of its **spores**. An infected ant will start losing its mind as the fungus fills its body and brain. The ant will wander aimlessly and fall down. Then, the fungus takes over completely. The unfortunate ant is forced to climb up the stem of a plant, find a perfect leaf, and CHOMP! The ant clamps its **mandibles** down on the underside of the leaf, where it eventually dies. All around it is a mass grave

Parasitic: depending on another organism for food or protection in a way that is usually harmful

Spores: tiny particles, similar to seeds, that allow fungi to reproduce

of other zombie ants that have already succumbed to the fungus, hanging directly above a trail of

Mandibles: like jaws, the strong parts of an insect's mouth that are used for biting

busy worker ants going about their business . . . for now, at least.

Ophiocordyceps changes the dead ant's internal organs into sugars that it can use to help itself grow. To protect itself from danger, it fills in any weak spots on the ant's outer shell. Finally, when the conditions are right for the fungus to continue its reproduction, a stalk pokes out . . . right through the dead ant's head! A round ball forms on the stalk, filled with more infectious spores. Eventually, the spores will rain down onto the unsuspecting ants below and the cycle will start again.

No more marching for this guy.

Scientists have found that the fungus does more than just control the ant's actions. It determines a final resting spot that will allow the fungus spores to thrive: not too hot, not too cold, and with just the right amount of light and moisture.

This location will also be near the ant colony, so the fungus can easily find new hosts and continue the cycle.

You might be wondering: Why doesn't the fungus just infect an ant and send it straight back to its nest to infect all the others right away? Well, for one thing, ants are very good at detecting threats and removing them from the nest. In addition, conditions inside the nest aren't ideal for the fungus to grow and reproduce. So forcing the infected ants to die *near* the nest—in a time and place perfect for the fungus to flourish—is a far better plan.

Zombie-making fungi won't be taking over the world anytime soon, though. Researchers have discovered that a given species of *Ophiocordyceps* can only infect a certain species of ants. In other words, the fungus can't control any old ant brain—it has to be just the right kind of ant brain or it won't work. And it turns out that there's yet another fungus that attacks the zombie fungus and keeps it from reproducing!

In a fungus-eat-fungus world, it looks like what goes around comes around.

Plant or Fungus— What's the Difference?

You might look at a mushroom growing out of the ground and conclude that mushrooms and other fungi are plants. In fact, for centuries biologists did just that. After all, fungi—like plants—don't move around much and are often found growing in the dirt. But there are some pretty big differences. First, plants make their own food from chlorophyll, sunlight, carbon dioxide, and water. But fungi can't do that. They need to eat something that is or was alive, such as a plant or animal. Also, the cell walls of plants are made of cellulose, while the cell walls of fungi are made of chitin—just like the shells of insects and crabs. Because of this, in 1969 the plant ecologist R. H. Whittaker proposed they be moved to their own kingdom (scientifically speaking, that is). Today, scientists have even come to believe that fungi are actually more closely related to animals than they are to plants. Who would have guessed?

CREEPY STUFF, RIGHT? *In this chapter you've explored a flower that smells (and sort of looks) like a corpse; the moss-creature hybrid known as slyrking; and a sinister parasite that turns regular ants into zombie slaves. Two of these stories are true—and the third is just a twisted tale. Which is which? The answers are out there. . . .*

A. WATCH YOUR STEP!

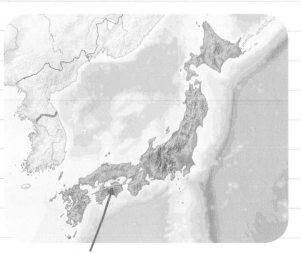

Iya River Valley

Crossing a bridge is no big deal, right? You probably do that fairly often. But how would you feel about walking on a bridge that was . . . *alive*?

In Japan there are living bridges made from vines of the wisteria plant. People carefully arrange the vines so that eventually they will

Don't look down!

grow all the way across a valley. No one knows for sure who built the first vine bridges or when, but several are still in use today. One of those is the Kazurabashi, a **suspension bridge** hanging over the secluded Iya River valley. At about 150 feet long, 6 feet wide, 45 feet above the water, and with only thin planks to walk on across the vines . . . you can imagine it might be pretty terrifying to cross! These days, though, you needn't worry quite as much: the bridge is now reinforced with steel cables and rebuilt every three years to keep it as safe as possible while still preserving its ancient feel.

> **Suspension bridge:** a bridge deck that hangs from ropes or cables that are supported by towers

In Indonesia, there is another kind of living bridge. Known

as Jembatan Akar (which means, literally, "root bridge"), it has spanned the Bayang River in West Sumatra for over a hundred years. The bridge is about five feet wide, over 80 feet long, and around 20 feet above the swift currents flowing beneath it. Legend has it that if you swim or bathe in the waters under the bridge, you will be granted a wish! Local lore says that the bridge was built—er, grown—by a teacher, Pakih Sohan, when he saw that his students on one side of the river couldn't get to their school on the other. There was a bamboo bridge, but the torrential currents frequently destroyed it and made the crossing dangerous or impossible. To solve this problem, the teacher is said to have planted a banyan tree on either bank, and gradually stretched the growing roots across a bamboo frame. After several years, the two trees' roots crossed each other in the middle and continued on to the other side. About twenty years later, the root bridge was finally strong enough for humans to cross, and much more durable than the bamboo bridges they'd used before. (Talk about planning ahead!) Today, the bridge is both a necessity for local residents and a highlight for visiting tourists.

Another living bridge, called the Umshiang Double Decker

Root Bridge, is probably the most famous one of all. It is located in northeastern India in the rainforest near Cherrapunji, which is known as the wettest place on Earth. People there have been weaving bridges out of tree roots for centuries. First, they hollow out the trunk of a betel nut tree and lay it across the river. Then, they thread the roots of a rubber tree (*Ficus elastica*) through the hollow trunk so that they will grow straight across the river. When the roots reach the other side, they are stuck back into the ground, where they continue growing! In this remote region of India, several root bridges have been constructed in this way.

Most modern bridges are made out of concrete and steel, which has to be manufactured and hauled in to the build site. Living bridges, on the other hand, take advantage of the materials at hand and the ingenuity of the people who live there to create something that is functional as well as beautiful.

Now that's green engineering!

Talk It Out

Humans have always been dependent on plants as a source of food, and we have found many other uses for them, too, including medicine and shelter. Brainstorm all of the different ways we use plants today. Can you think of any problems that could result from any of those uses? What new uses might we come up with in the future?

B. LET THERE BE FLOWER POWER!

Have you ever woken up in the middle of the night to a completely pitch-black house? The bedroom is dark. The hallway is dark. The bathroom is dark. You can barely see your hands as you fumble around trying to find the light switch. Well, what if the fix for all this darkness was as simple as . . . a potted plant? Bioluminescence is a fancy word that means "something alive that gives off light." The light comes from the mixing of two organic materials called *luciferase* and *luciferin*. You might have seen evidence of this in some insects, such as fireflies and glowworms. Under the sea, there's the lantern fish, the flashlight fish, and the gulper eel. In the plant world, though, bioluminescence is a lot harder to find.

But it's not impossible. As far back as 1751, legendary Swedish naturalist Carolus

Naturalist
Carolus Linnaeus

Linnaeus designed an ingenious plan for a "flower clock." This involved growing a specific group of flowers, each of which opened its petals at a specific hour of the day, so that you could tell the time according to which flowers were open or closed. The midnight hour on Linnaeus's flower clock was marked by the western moonflower, or *Ipomoea alba lucifera*. Special features? A gentle glow lasting up to an hour after the blooms first open. As the sun rises, the blooms close again, leaving the flower dormant until the following evening.

The western moonflower enjoyed a brief burst of fame in 1931, when *Life* magazine included it in a feature on fascinating plants. Despite its popularity, though, the plant proved tough to cultivate. In the wild, the six to eight blooms on each plant, clustered together, give off a dim but visible light. But in the greenhouse or the laboratory, the light given off is faint and barely visible to the human eye. And, of course, it is only truly visible during the

Re-creation of Carolus Linnaeus's flower clock

midnight hour when the blooms open.

Tricky little moonflower!

Over the last two decades, botanists have been hard at work trying to understand the western moonflower's **luminosity**, and to discover how they might replicate it—or harness it for practical use. Because it's so much dimmer outside of its natural habitat, scientists think that its light-giving properties might come in part through pollination by bioluminescent insects. But tests are still ongoing; so far, the western moonflower is keeping its secrets. "We haven't given up, not by a long

Western moonflower in full glow!

Luminosity: glow

shot," says Harper Nugabwe, a biologist at Stanford University. "Solving this puzzle could have an incredible impact on global energy."

Either way, bioluminescent plants remain on the cutting edge of modern **horticulture**. Dutch innovator Daan Roosegaarde is experimenting with genetically modifying plants' molecular structures to add luciferin as a way to create bioluminescence. But any genetic modifications can be risky: How will the resulting **cross-pollination** affect other plants? Will there be any harm to existing species? What are the environmental risks?

Horticulture: the study of plants

Cross-pollination: when pollen from one plant is carried to another

Scientists such as Nugabwe who are studying the moonflower hope that their experiments can bring long-term solutions without the risks of genetic modification. If so, the results could be far-reaching. Imagine waking up in the pitch-dark middle of the night. Outside your window, the night is the cold hard black of coal. But just inside the glass, on your windowsill, sits a potted plant—a plant blooming with small white flowers. It's past midnight, so each flower glows warm and gentle, a living night-light just when you need it most.

Endangered Plants?

Did you know that plants can go extinct, just like animals? In fact, habitat destruction—whether from human activity or global climate change—can be even more devastating for plants than for animals, since plants can't easily move to a better location. Also, since humans have taken over the cultivation of many species, their diversity has been severely restricted, leaving those plants more vulnerable than ever to pests and diseases. The International Union for Conservation of Nature (IUCN) has evaluated 12,914 species of plants and found that a whopping 68% of them are currently in danger of extinction. Since most life on Earth depends on plants for food, shelter, and oxygen, that's a big, fat, scary deal!

Fortunately, there are initiatives in place to try to help. Many organizations, such as the Nature Conservancy, are working around the world to protect natural habitats—for plants as well as for animals. Groups like IUCN's own Plants Conservation Sub-Committee lead efforts to slow the loss of plant diversity worldwide through networks of plant conservationists. And seed banks like the Millennium Seed Bank in Wakehurst, England, are storing seeds from species that are in danger of going extinct in the wild to ensure that we don't lose those plants forever.

We all know that eating too much sugar is bad for us. But it just tastes so good; sometimes we don't want to stop! Wouldn't it be great if we could make *everything* we eat taste deliciously sweet without having to worry about calories or cavities? Someday soon, there may be an all-natural way to do just that.

Introducing . . . the miracle fruit!

Agbayun, otherwise known as *Synsepalum dulcificum*, grows naturally in tropical parts of Ghana, West Africa, on an evergreen bush that can reach up to 16 feet tall. The fruit is a bright-red, football-shaped berry that grows to be about an inch long. For centuries, West African people have eaten agbayun

Ghana

berries before they consume beer, wine, or sour-tasting **gruel**.

What's the scoop? Well, this miracle fruit has the strange ability to make any foods eaten after it, especially sour ones, taste perfectly sweet! But how does it work? That's what scientists have been trying to figure out.

Agbayun berries

They've learned that the miracle fruit contains a protein, appropriately named miraculin. Miraculin by itself doesn't taste like much of anything, but it binds to the cells in our taste buds—called receptors—that process sweet flavors. When we're not eating or drinking anything **acidic**, miraculin blocks those receptors so we can't taste things that are actually sweet. But when we eat or drink something acidic or sour, like lemons, the miraculin changes shape and activates the taste bud receptors for sweet. This tricks our brains into thinking we've just eaten something sweet instead of something sour.

Gruel: a thin food made by boiling grain in water

Acidic: sour or sharp tasting

The more sour the food, the stronger the reaction will be . . . and the sweeter it will taste! The miraculin stays on the tongue and continues to affect the taste buds for half an hour or more after eating it.

Many people have wondered if we can find a way to use

Take Action

Many threatened and endangered plants need our help (and we need them, too)! What can we do as individuals to help protect plants, now and in the future? What can we do as groups of concerned individuals joining together? What can we do as cities, nations, or globally? Brainstorm different actions that you could take, then choose one and start doing it!

miraculin to solve problems. Maybe it could be used to help people with **diabetes** eat less sugar without giving up on taste? Or, perhaps there could be a way to reduce world hunger by making plentiful but unappetizing food, like bitter grasses or greens, taste better? Unfortunately, miracle fruit doesn't grow very well outside of tropical West Africa, so it has been difficult to produce miraculin in large quantities. Modern science might soon

Diabetes: a disease in which the body cannot process sugar normally

Would you try it?

find a way to solve that, however, as researchers are now experimenting with ways to grow miraculin in indoor forms or even inside everyday foods like tomatoes or lettuce.

We'll have to wait and see just how miraculin will be used, but one thing is for sure . . . when life gives you lemons, miracle fruit can make them taste like lemonade!

THE PLANT WORLD IS *pretty wild! You've just read about enormous bridges that are actual living plant structures; a type of flower you could use as a night-light; and a miracle fruit that makes sour things eaten after it taste super sweet. What are the truths? What is the lie? Careful research will tell!*

PART 2

ASTONISHING ANIMALS— SMALL, MEDIUM, LARGE

The animal kingdom is a rich and fascinating place. With over eight million animal species on Earth, there is more than enough to keep any curious learners busy until the end of their days.

And we're willing to bet that no matter how much you learn about the animal world, these creatures will *still* find ways to surprise you.

If you've read Part 1 of this book, you're already getting the idea for how this works. Read on and prepare to unhinge your jaws. . . .

A. PUPPY'S GOT A BRAND-NEW PAL

Everybody needs a friend, right? Someone to talk to. Someone to do stuff with. Someone who can curl up quietly and snooze inside your ear until the next time you want to hang out.

Wait—what?

Okay, maybe that last one's not the most common thing for a friend to do. But if you were a wild dog in East Africa, your closest pal might just be a tiny creature called an African threadsnake, which would live—you guessed it!—inside your ear.

The African threadsnake (or *Leptotyphlops rakae*) is a species of blind threadsnake that is native to the East African countries of

Kenya and Tanzania, though specimens have been spotted as far east as the island of Madagascar. The tiny snakes only ever grow one to two inches long, making them the smallest snake on record. They're thin, too: barely fatter  than a string of spaghetti! With their glistening pink bodies, they are often mistaken for tiny earthworms.

But that's not what you want to hear about, is it? Okay, okay. What's extraordinary about the African threadsnake is that its natural habitat is inside the

Domesticated: not wild; cared for by people

middle ear canal of wild dogs. African wild dogs are quite different from their **domesticated** cousins. Their ears are large and cone-shaped, and they have sharp eyes and distinctive, spotted coats that help them blend in with their scrubby landscape. In domestic dogs, the middle ear chamber is a small area containing three tiny bones and sealed off by the eardrum. But wild dogs have something extra: a tiny passage leading into that

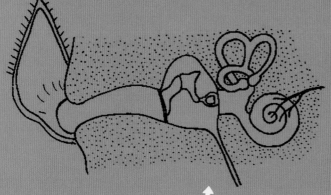

Diagram of a threadsnake's home: a canine's inner ear

chamber from the outer ear.

This tiny open ear space is where the threadsnake makes its home.

What do threadsnakes eat, you wonder? The major part of their diet consists of . . . earwax! This goopy substance is mostly made up of discarded skin cells and oils from the skin's outer layer. This gives the threadsnakes just about all they need to survive, and through their discreet munching, they keep their hosts' ear canals clean as a dinner plate. So: food aplenty for the threadsnakes, and improved hearing for their dog hosts. Win-win!

African wild dogs are currently endangered, but **herpetologists** have noticed that life expectancy is greater for those dogs that play host to the threadsnakes. Better hearing means sharper reflexes,

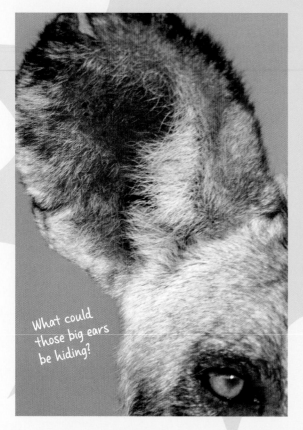

What could those big ears be hiding?

and scientists think this might give these wild dogs an extra edge to help them survive and thrive in an increasingly hostile world.

"The African threadsnake is the most exciting new species to be discovered in the last decade," says Jarvis Adeoye, a researcher at the HERP Project (Herpetology Education in Rural Places and Spaces), a National Science Foundation project. Adeoye and his team have set up a base outside Mombasa in hopes of learning more about these tiny creatures—and their hosts—and to see what can be done to enhance both of their livelihoods.

Still, the wild dog population continues to dwindle, and with it hope for the African threadsnakes' own survival. Despite all efforts of the HERP team, the

Herpetologists: scientists who study snakes

Symbiotic: a relationship between two parties from which both benefit

threadsnakes stubbornly refuse to thrive anywhere outside the ears of their canine companions. "It's an evolutionary **symbiotic** bond that has grown exceptionally strong," Adeoye says. Some scientists have wondered whether certain types of domestic dogs might be bred to carry the threadsnakes, but this is just speculation.

For the time being, the fate of the African threadsnake is uncertain. But on the savannas of Kenya and Tanzania, these tiny interlopers still ride free, curled up inside their closest companions in the world. Dog and snake, snake and dog, together—and that's all that matters.

Try This!

New creatures are being discovered every day. Choose an existing animal with a specific habitat, then speculate about what kinds of variations of that animal might one day be discovered. Where would each live, why, and how would that creature be different from those we know today? Illustrate one of the new animals and its habitat.

B. THE TINY GUARDIANS OF YOUR BOOKSHELF

Imagine you could shrink yourself down, right now—ziiiiip!—and slip into a book. Not actually falling into a story, like the kids who were sucked into Narnia through a painting in *The Voyage of the Dawn Treader*, but squashing yourself down to, say, the size of this capital letter B. And then going for a stroll across the pages of one of those dusty old books in your grandfather's library.

If you did this, you just might find yourself in the path of a very startling creature: Meet the book scorpion, better known as the house pseudoscorpion, or *Chelifer cancroides*. These microscopic arachnids look a lot like regular scorpions, with eight legs and two long, front-reaching pincers. But there are two big differences. First,

A close-up look at the intrepid book scorpion

book scorpions have no stinging tails. And second, they are teeny-tiny (unless you're shrunk down to their size, of course). A third of an inch is as big as they're ever going to grow.

And why do you suppose they're called book scorpions?

Well, they love books, of course!

Book scorpions can sneak into your library in many ways, but one of their favorite methods is playing tag-along. The tiny pseudoscorpion clings to the leg of a fly or other insect, then drops off when indoors. Once the book scorpion reaches a bookshelf, its hunt for food begins. The tiny predator is not too picky: dust mites, moth or beetle larvae, and—drumroll, please!—book lice.

What are book lice, you ask? They are insects, even tinier than book scorpions, that devour books. Specifically, book lice love to eat the starchy glue that holds old books together. So, like the excellent bookshelf guardians they are, book scorpions come along and eat the book lice before the book lice can eat your books. Gulp. Yum! Whew.

Pseudoscorpions have been around a long time—they were mentioned in the writings of the philosopher Aristotle, who lived way back around 300 BCE. Still, most people today have never heard of them. For one thing, they are timid creatures and spend most of their time lurking out of sight. And, of course, they're as small as the words printed on this page. You might walk by their

Great Groups!

Each of these has been used to refer to a group of animals, except one.

1. Hissing of snakes
2. Aurora of polar bears
3. Embarrassment of pandas
4. Bouquet of pheasants
5. Murder of crows
6. Squad of squid
7. Implausibility of gnus
8. Zeal of zebras
9. Gulp of magpies
10. Confusion of guinea fowl

hiding spots every single day and never get a glimpse.

Unless you were the right size, of course. Then you'd be able to meet and get to know this fascinating creature: your bookshelf's very own guardian and defender.

MIGHTY MOLLUSKS

C.

Behold the lowly limpet!

Sure, the small species of sea snail known as *Patella vulgata* may not look like much. It doesn't seem to *do* very much, either. But this mighty **mollusk**, better known as the common European limpet, has some terrifically tough teeth. And those little limpet teeth might someday help us build stronger race-car bodies, bridges, rocket ships, and more! How, you ask? Well . . .

A limpet eats by dragging its **radula** over the tops of

Mollusk: a classification of animals with soft bodies (and usually hard shells), such as snails, clams, and squid

A common European limpet

rocks, and its hundreds of tiny teeth scrape off the algae and **diatoms** that grow there. Limpet teeth must be able to withstand the super-scratchy surface of the rocks without breaking off or wearing down too much. In other words, they have to be strong.

Professor Asa Barber, from the University of Portsmouth, has been studying these seemingly simple creatures, and he recently made a startling discovery: those little limpet teeth are not just strong—they're actually the strongest biological material ever discovered! Barber started by looking at tensile strength, which is a measure of how much force is needed to pull something apart until it breaks. He

Extreme close-up of some tough stuff!

Radula: A tough, tonguelike band with teeth

Diatoms: small floating algae common in fresh and salt water that have cell walls made of silica

Gigapascal: one billion pascals, the standard unit of measurement of pressure

found that limpet teeth have a tensile strength of 6.5 **gigapascals** (GPa), which is about the same as the strongest carbon fibers ever made by humans. Spider silk, which was previously thought to be the strongest natural material in the world, has a tensile strength of 4.5 GPa. For comparison, Kevlar, the synthetic material used to make bulletproof body armor, is only 3 to 3.5 GPa. And human teeth? Not even close.

Chitin: the hard substance that makes up the shells of many insects and crustaceans

Goethite: a common brown mineral that is the main component in many types of rust

Barber wanted to know what makes limpet teeth so strong. He discovered that they are a composite material, a substance that's made up of two or more

Trails made by feeding limpets

ingredients with significantly different physical or chemical properties. Each limpet tooth has an internal framework made of **chitin**. Closely packed nanofibers, microscopic strands of a hard iron-oxide mineral known as **goethite**, fill in that framework. Together, the chitin and the goethite are what give limpet teeth their amazing strength.

It also gives them another very interesting quality. Unlike most structures, limpet teeth seem to be just as strong no matter what their size. "Generally, a big structure has lots of flaws and can break more easily than a smaller structure, which has fewer flaws and is stronger," Barber says. But limpet teeth seem to break this rule. The diameter of the nanofibers seems to be small enough that flaws just don't matter, so large structures made from them can be every bit as strong as smaller ones.

Crazy Creatures from Under the Sea

Can you guess which one of these ocean-dwelling animals is the fake?

1. Pink see-through fantasia
2. Christmas tree worm
3. Flamingo tongue snail
4. Layabout lobster
5. Vampire squid
6. Leafy sea dragon
7. Fathead
8. Spiny lumpsucker
9. Dumbo octopus
10. Gold-lace nudibranch

Now scientists can start copying limpet teeth to create new and better materials for building and manufacturing. Imagine that one day you go to the dentist to get a cavity filled, and the material your filling is made of mimics that of a limpet tooth!

Chewing on rocks, however, would still not be recommended.

COULDN'T YOU JUST READ *about critters all day long? The cuties you've learned about in this chapter include a tiny threadsnake that has a symbiotic best friendship with a species of wild dog; nearly microscopic pseudoscorpions that guard your bookshelf; and the underwater limpet, whose teeth are its superpower. One is false . . . two are true. You know what to do!*

A. INVASION OF THE TREE OCTOPODS

Quick, name three facts about the octopus: eight legs . . . powerful beak . . . lives in the ocean? All true of your average octopus.

But what happens when you come across an octopus that *isn't* quite so average? Just over two decades ago, naturalists were excited to discover an entirely new type of octopod—one that challenged some key things scientists had grown to expect in the species. The newcomer is known scientifically as *Octopus paxarbolis*, or more commonly as the Pacific Northwest tree octopus.

An octopus . . . . in a tree!

Yep, that's right: An octopus. That lives in trees.

First discovered by respected naturalist Lyle Zapato in 1998, the tree octopus has evolved to make its home deep in the rainforests of Washington State's Olympic Peninsula. It moves using its powerful suckers to anchor to its tree of choice. You won't find the tree octopus swinging around during the day, though. The night is when it likes to venture out to hunt, feeding on rodents, frogs, and other small mammals. In exceptionally hot or dry weather, the tree octopus will make frequent trips to nearby bodies of water to cool and replenish its naturally moist hide. During the height of the rainy season, though, it can easily live on land for weeks at a time.

The tree octopus is a timid

Looks like octopus is on the menu. . . .

and solitary creature, living alone and camouflaging itself into its surroundings. It's also got a remarkably advanced brain capacity, which is opening up new avenues for science. What interesting information might this aquatic tree dweller be able to share, if only it could be understood?

While the tree octopus spends most of its life outside of water, it returns to the ocean to lay its eggs. The tiny hatchlings spend their first weeks underwater, growing in size and strength. Finally they clamber up onto the

Talk It Out

A "grassroots" movement is one that is started by everyday people—just like you. What are the strengths of this type of movement? Do you have something you're passionate about that you think needs changing? What are some things you could do about it?

banks and head for the safety of the trees, where they will live out the rest of their lives.

In the early 2000s, the tree octopus was on the verge of **extinction**, but a strong grassroots campaign by dedicated Pacific Northwest communities helped reverse that. They set about raising awareness and establishing "**cephalopod**-safe" forest zones. The result? The tree octopus has seen a terrific comeback, and is now one of the fastest-growing octopod species on the West Coast.

Extinction: when the last of a species dies out

Cephalopod: any mollusk with tentacles

So, if you're out and about on a gray, rainy day, keep your eyes on those treetops! Maybe *you'll* be the one to spot something unusual lurking in their boughs.

B. THE EXTRAORDINARY, EXTRA-CRANIAL LIFE OF MIKE

Our story begins in the fall of 1945. Lloyd Olsen and his wife ran a small family farm in Fruita, Colorado. Among other things, the Olsen farm specialized in chickens. It was Lloyd Olsen's routine, once a week, to behead a batch of birds with an ax, then load the carcasses into his wagon for delivery to the meat market the next morning.

But on the fateful day of September 10, things didn't go as planned: not for Olsen, and certainly not for the plump, 2.5-pound chicken who was earmarked for the next day's dinner.

Just like every Monday, Olsen raised the ax.

Just like every Monday, the blade fell.

Now, it's not uncommon for a chicken to continue running around for a bit after its head is chopped off. So when the feisty bird kept gamboling around, the farmer probably wasn't too

Lloyd Olsen and Mike the chicken

surprised. He relegated the headless body to an apple crate on the porch and turned in for the night. The next morning, though, Olsen was in for a shock.

The chicken was still alive!

It had no head, but it was very clearly not dead. What happened? It turned out that Olsen's ax had missed the bird's **jugular vein**, so the blood clotted and the flow stopped quickly. The ax had also missed severing the **brain stem**, and with that organ intact, the chicken, who became known as Mike, was able to maintain much of his behavior. He began "pecking at the ground for food with his newly minted stump, and made preening motions. His crows had become throaty gurglings," reported the journal *Scientific American* in its 2014 feature on the fated fowl.

In the face of this

Jugular vein: the main blood vessel in the neck or throat

Brain stem: lower part of the brain, which manages things like breathing, swallowing, and consciousness

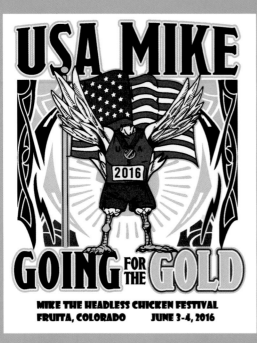

USA MIKE

GOING FOR THE GOLD

MIKE THE HEADLESS CHICKEN FESTIVAL
FRUITA, COLORADO   JUNE 3-4, 2016

tenacity, you might not be surprised at what Olsen decided to do next. Armed with an eyedropper, the man set about the task of helping Mike stay alive, painstakingly delivering water, milk, and even tiny corn kernels directly into the bird's **esophagus**.

The result? Mike not only lived but thrived. At the University of Utah, Mike was poked and prodded and finally given a clean bill of health: against all odds, he lived on. Over the next eighteen months, in fact, Mike nearly quadrupled his body weight to a hefty eight pounds. Mike would go on to be featured in *Time* and *Life* magazines, and even made the Guinness World Records book. (Can you guess for what?)

Spurred on by flocks of incredulous inquiries, Lloyd Olsen decided to take his miracle chicken on the road. On the sideshow circuit, the Olsens and Mike traveled from their hometown in Colorado through California, Arizona, New York, and beyond, where people

Esophagus: the channel linking the throat to the stomach

of all ages could pay 25 cents to see Mike, the Miracle Chicken.

Eventually, of course, Mike did meet his end. But his legacy lives on in the annual Mike the Headless Chicken Festival (held the first weekend in June), and in the four-foot-high sculpture of Mike that was installed in downtown Fruita in early 2000. More than 70 years later, the curious and thunderstruck alike still remember this noble bird who exchanged a quick trip to the platter for a blazing streak of national fame.

Animals: Fact or Fake?

All of these are true, except for one! Can you figure out the fake?

1. Turtles can breathe out of their butts.

2. Some octopuses have three hearts.

3. Scorpions can survive being frozen inside a block of ice.

4. Vultures sometimes eat too much to fly, so they throw up.

5. Mother giraffes give birth standing up, so newborn giraffes fall about five feet down to the ground.

6. Jellyfish poop through their mouths.

7. Horses often throw up their food hours after eating, just so they can eat it again.

8. Geckos don't have any eyelids, so they clean their eyes by licking them.

9. Crows pull the tails of other animals, often to distract them and steal their food.

10. Bats can have sparkly poop.

OLMY GOODNESS, TINY DRAGONS!

C.

What's your favorite kind of pet: A roly-poly kitten, maybe? Or an energetic, tail-wagging German shepherd? Or a delicate goldfish in a bowl? Maybe even a slow-moving box turtle? Those are all great pets. But have you ever thought about having your own personal . . . dragon?

Curious to know more? C'mon, let's go on an adventure. For this trip you'll need warm clothes, sturdy boots, and a flashlight with a strong beam. We're going to travel to the Eastern European country of Slovenia. Deep in the mountains, in the aquatic caves of Postojna, lives a species of cave-dwelling salamander that looks just like a baby dragon. It's known as *Proteus anguinus* or, more informally, the olm.

Now, let's be honest. You're not going to take an olm home with you. They are aquatic cave dwellers, after all. But why don't you stick around for a while anyway; our tour is just getting started. Want to get up close and personal with a real-life pocket dragon? Here we go.

Olms can grow to be eight to 12 inches long (about the length of your forearm), with slithery snakelike bodies and slender limbs. They have three toes on each of their forelegs and just two toes on their hind legs. Basically? They look exactly like a tiny baby dragon! They have three pink fanlike **gills** on either side of their head, and their pale, fleshy skin is so thin that you can see through to the shapes of their internal organs!

Gills: fleshy openings through which aquatic animals breathe

They are born with underdeveloped eyes that, within months of their birth, become almost completely blind. Many olms' eyes are grown over with a thin layer of skin, though they can still register changes in light around them. As if to make up for this, olms' other senses are supercharged: smell, taste, and especially hearing. They can detect the smallest sound waves and microdisturbances in the water around them. Olms also have a weird sixth sense: electro-sensitivity. A special organ in their heads helps them detect electrical waves of passing creatures. Is that a tiny sea worm? Gulp! All gone.

Mealtime for the olm consists of insects and small aquatic creatures such as crabs and water snails. Food can be scarce in the dark bellies of the caves that serve as their homes, so when they

Charles Darwin

find food, they gobble up as much of it as they can. They can then store these nutrients in their bodies for another hungry day. How long? For up to 10 years! Since an olm might live as long as 100 years, that's not very many mealtimes.

Historical records of the olm date back to 1768. They were further immortalized by Charles Darwin in *On the Origin of Species* as an example of an ancient organism shaped by its harsh environment.

You can find the olm primarily in the southeastern European countries of Slovenia, Croatia, and Bosnia and Herzegovina. In Slovenia they are considered a national treasure, and their image was printed on one of their 10-stotin coins. Dragon treasure, anyone?

In Slovenia, for the equivalent of about 20 dollars, you can board a special train that will take you through the Postojna cave for an up-close-and-personal tour.

ON

THE ORIGIN OF SPECIES

BY MEANS OF NATURAL SELECTION,

OR THE

PRESERVATION OF FAVOURED RACES IN THE STRUGGLE
FOR LIFE.

BY CHARLES DARWIN, M.A.,

FELLOW OF THE ROYAL, GEOLOGICAL, LINNÆAN, ETC., SOCIETIES;
AUTHOR OF 'JOURNAL OF RESEARCHES DURING H. M. S. BEAGLE'S VOYAGE
ROUND THE WORLD.'

LONDON:
JOHN MURRAY, ALBEMARLE STREET.
1859.

The right of Translation is reserved.

Yep—olms were mentioned in here!

You can't take one of these baby dragons home, but—isn't the world a better place just because you know the olm is in it?

Take Action

- Find a patch of grass or dirt where you can get comfortable. Focus on a small section, about one foot by one foot square, and observe it carefully for 10 minutes. Write down everything you notice. You might be surprised to see just how much is going on down there!

- Are there any endangered animal species living near you? Do some research and learn about these animals and how human involvement might help in their protection and preservation. Then choose one and start a campaign to raise awareness of its plight. You could draw posters, create a blog, write a letter to the editor or a press release for your local newspaper, prepare a presentation for your class . . . you decide! No bit of help is too small.

MORE MID-SIZED ANIMALS . . . *more fun! This chapter introduced you to a daring species of tree-living octopus; a chicken from the last century that lived long after being beheaded; and a species of small "dragons" still alive today. We wish they were all true—but only two of these stories have that honor! Can you find out which ones?*

A. DISCOVERING PREHISTORIC BAMBI

Summer vacation—woohoo! That means it's time to go to the beach . . . play tons of online games . . . laze around in the sun and spend the whole day doing nothing . . . go digging for fossils!

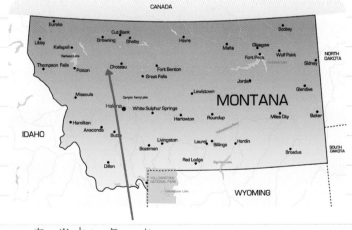

Two Medicine Formation

Hold on. What was that last one?

If you had grown up as part of the Linster family of Stevensville, Montana, "summer vacation" would mean something quite different to you than it does to most people. Starting back in the mid-1980s, when their seven children were small, the Linster family developed a common passion: **paleontology**. In what

Paleontology: the science of studying fossilized plants and animals

became a yearly tradition, the start of summer saw Cliff and Sandy Linster packing up their family for the three-hour drive to a plot of land on the Rocky Mountain Front known as Two Medicine Formation.

What did they do once they got there? They all began to dig.

Out came their tools, things like trowels and shovels and screens, hand brooms and dustpans and tape measures. Year in and year out—from the time the Linster kids were very young—the family spent their summers camping and excavating their rented plot of land, looking for a very particular type of treasure: dinosaur bones!

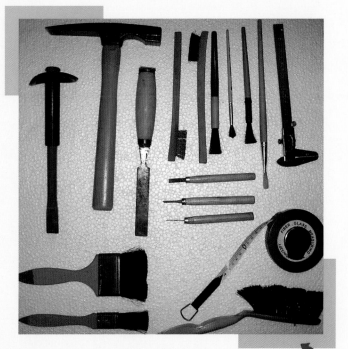

A paleontologist's tools of the trade

And boy, did they find them. Over the years, the Linster family unearthed over 8,000 different bones. But it was what happened in the summer of 1994 that would change everything—and make paleontological history. On that day, 14-year-old Wes was working on a hilly section of land when something caught his eye.

Bones! Could those be . . . teeth? A jaw?

Already an experienced excavator, Wes knew he was seeing something special. Together with his parents, he uncovered what would prove to be the skeleton of an entirely new species of raptor—and one that was nearly perfectly preserved. With over 90% of its bones intact, this turned out to be one of the most complete raptor skeletons discovered in the whole United States.

Like its discoverer, the new dinosaur was just a kid. The Linster family nicknamed it "Bambi," and the name stuck. Now known

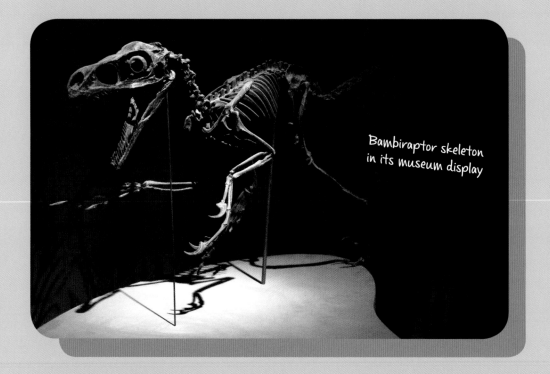

Bambiraptor skeleton in its museum display

as the *Bambiraptor feinbergi*, the three-foot-long juvenile dinosaur (estimated to be four feet long when fully grown) stood upright, had a birdlike body and long spindly arms, and possessed quite a large brain. With a big claw on its second toe, the late Cretaceous-era dinosaur is thought to have been a fierce hunter. Experts think the *Bambiraptor* fed on small reptiles and mammals—maybe even stealing baby duck-billed dinosaurs right out of their nests, according to University of Kansas paleontologist David Burnham.

In 2002, the *Bambiraptor* skeleton went on display in Kansas University's Biodiversity Institute and Natural History Museum in Lawrence, Kansas. There, many thousands of visitors pass through every year. And each visitor has the chance to see, up close and personal, this baby dinosaur discovered by an amateur kid paleontologist—maybe not much older than you.

It kind of makes you reconsider your plans for next summer vacation, doesn't it?

Actual Dinosaur Names (or Are They?)

All but one of them is. . . .

1. Irritator challengeri
2. Gasosaurus
3. Arthurdactylus conandoylensis
4. Camelotia borealis
5. Dracorex hogwarsia
6. Bookasaurus longuous
7. Elvisaurus
8. Supersaurus
9. Gigantoraptor
10. Technosaurus

B. MEGACONDA— MYTH NO MORE

Bigfoot, el chupacabra, the Loch Ness Monster, the yeti: all of these are cryptids, animals that may exist but that haven't yet been verified and documented by the scientific community. Have you ever dreamed of finding one and proving that it was real? In a combination of scientific exploration and lucky timing, some British citizens recently did just that.

The giant anaconda has long been considered to be a cryptid. No hard evidence for its existence had ever been found, despite the fact that rumors of the huge snake—also known as the "brown

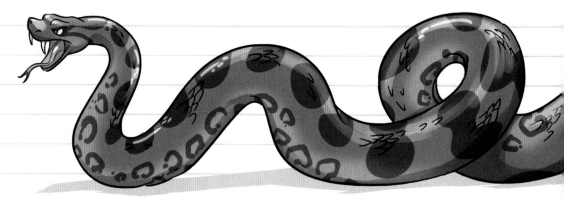

82 feet—as long as two school buses!

boa" or yacumama—have been around for as long as people have. According to local legend in the Amazon River basin in Brazil, a yacumama can swallow any living thing that comes within a hundred yards of it. **Indigenous** people who live there still blow on a **conch** horn before entering the water in hopes of scaring away any yacumamas that may be hiding in the murky waters.

Colonel Fawcett, before he disappeared

In 1906, the Royal Geographical Society in London sent explorer Colonel Percy Fawcett to map that area of Brazil. He claimed to have shot a giant anaconda 62 feet long and 12 inches in diameter, much bigger than any snake ever previously recorded.

But he offered no proof. Fawcett later returned to the same area in 1925 to look for more giant anacondas, but before he could prove their existence . . . he vanished without a trace.

Amateur cryptid hunter

Indigenous: originating from or living naturally in a particular region

Conch: a shell from a large sea snail

Mike Warner knew all the stories. He'd been studying reports of the giant anaconda for 23 years. It was the dream of a lifetime when, at age 73, he took a trip to try to find them. The hunt would take Warner and his son, Greg, from their home in Ireland to the Amazon River basin in South America. With the help of Jose Valles Padilla, an experienced guide and translator, and Jorge Pinedo, a local pilot with over 30 years of experience, father and son spent 12 days in early 2015 surveying the rainforest.

The team set off in a hydroplane with a video camera mounted on each side. Greg Warner shot hundreds of

The Amazon River

This is what it would look like next to a jeep!

still photos. Seeing a giant anaconda seemed like too much to hope for. After all, it's unusual to even spot the smaller common green anaconda in the wild, since they spend most of their time in the water. A giant anaconda would be especially likely to stay in the water due to its tremendous weight, and the waters of the Amazon are muddy and brown—perfect for concealing an enormous brown boa!

Mike Warner and his team went in looking for a specific type of evidence: channels. "When Colonel Fawcett first went to the Amazon, he documented large trails six feet wide made by the giant snakes as they move about the swampy ground," says Warner. "We wanted to find the channels as proof that the snakes exist." And they were elated to find several such channels. Then, things got even more exciting. A giant anaconda approached the surface of the river just as they were flying over, and Greg Warner was able to snap some photos before it disappeared again beneath the surface!

Based on the photos, herpetologists estimate the snake to be about 82 feet long, to measure almost a yard in diameter, and to weigh more than a ton—almost four times as large as any other snake on record. And judging by the number of channels documented, the Warners' giant anaconda isn't alone out there, either. Biologists are now mounting several expeditions in the coming years to try to learn more about the giant anaconda and observe it in the wild—from a safe distance, of course!

And Mike Warner? He's thrilled to have finally proven that the megaconda is more than just a myth after all.

Talk It Out

How does an animal's environment shape its growth and development? How might two members of the same species, raised in different environments, eventually evolve differently? Why?

C. GELATINOUS CURTAIN OF DEATH

It's an animal! It's a machine! It's . . . a superorganism!

Can you name the largest animal on Earth? If you said the blue whale, you're right. But what about the longest animal on Earth? That is something else entirely.

Meet *Praya dubia*, one of many species of sea creatures known as siphonophores, which are related to animals like jellyfish, corals,

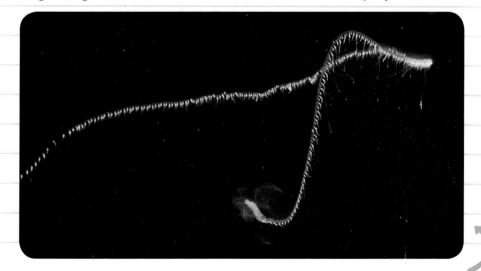

Want a closer look at this
Praya dubia? Better not!

A Marrus siphonophore, photographed at 5,250 feet below the surface

and sea anemones. Blue whales have been known to grow over 100 feet long and weigh almost 200 tons, but *Praya dubia* can stretch to 130 feet or more . . . yet they weigh comparatively little!

Siphonophores have been called superorganisms, because each "one" isn't actually a single animal at all. Instead, it's a whole colony of individuals that live and work closely together. You can think of it as being something like an anthill with each of the ants playing its part, except in this case the anthill itself is alive! Each member of the colony has a specialized job to do, such as swimming, reproducing, or feeding. Together, they work like the parts of a machine or the cells in a body, each individual depending on the others to function as a single, complete organism.

And where do all those individuals come from? Instead of a

male and female reproducing together and giving birth or laying eggs, a single siphonophore simply sprouts clones of itself. The clones then join the larger organism and get to work. In our anthill example, that would be like the anthill itself being able to produce more ants!

There are other unusual things about siphonophores, too. Siphonophores seem to do just fine without having a brain, heart, gills, or lungs. Most don't have eyes, yet they can somehow sense light and dark. They don't have a protective shell, yet they manage to defend themselves. They may be able to direct their own movement and find food. Some can emit light to attract prey, and most—including *Praya dubia*—are venomous, making them deadly predators.

The body of *Praya dubia* is only as thick around as a rope, squishy and fragile, and mostly transparent, but its "arms" pack a deadly punch. Like most siphonophores, *Praya dubia* drifts gracefully along through the deep ocean waters. But dangling beneath it is a net of stinging tentacles that it uses to catch— and kill—its dinner: fish, crustaceans, jellyfish, and even other siphonophores. Despite the lack of sharp teeth and tough skin, scientists now think siphonophores play a much bigger role in their food webs than they ever dreamed possible. It seems likely that these strange creatures are even capable of outcompeting other formidable ocean predators like sharks and whales!

Studying these unusual ocean animals—which kind of resemble living snot—hasn't been easy. Their soft bodies are often destroyed when biologists use nets and other traditional ways to try to catch them, and they may spontaneously break apart when they are brought up to the surface. Some even seem to self-destruct when exposed to bright light! Fortunately, technology is improving, and if researchers

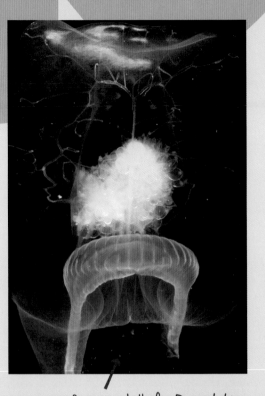

Swimming bell of a *Praya dubia*, photographed thanks to research done by the Monterey Bay Aquarium Research Institute

can't bring the creatures to a lab, perhaps they can bring the lab to them. Marine biologists are now using submersible research vessels and ROVs (remotely operated vehicles) to get up close and personal with siphonophores in their natural habitats. And cameras can now take quality photos using much less light than they used to. All of these developments are helping us study a species we don't really know much about.

We do know that *Praya dubia* prefers to live in extremely deep waters, and that seems like a very good thing. Superorganism or not, I wouldn't want to run into one next time I'm at the beach. Would you?

Try This!

- The deep ocean is one of the most mysterious places on Earth, with new species of creatures being discovered all the time. Pretend you are a deep-sea explorer who has just come upon an astonishing new creature. What does it look like? Where does it live? What does it eat? How does it protect itself? Make sure to give your creature a name and sketch its portrait for posterity!

- Wish you could go someplace new and see surprising and unusual things for yourself? Shake off the blahs by doing a little research to learn what interesting or unusual things are offered right in your own area. Dogsled racing? Sailing tall ships? Volunteering at horse stables? You'll never know what fun things might be just around the corner until you look!

BIGGER AND BIGGER AND *bigger they grew! You've now learned all about the discovery of a young dinosaur named after Bambi; the mythical megaconda, finally caught on camera; and a creepy 100-foot-long creature that lives deep in the ocean. Which ones can you believe? With just a little research the truths will be revealed. . . .*

PART 3

HOW ABOUT HUMANS—
YES! NOOOO. MAYBE?

Plants, animals . . . What could be next? Well, how does humanity rate on the scale of important topics in science? Fairly high, we think!

This section of the book will focus on human biology, including some unbelievable experiences, fascinating discoveries, amazing inventions, and more.

Be they past, present, or possibly in the very near future, get ready to read some stories that will shake your sense of reality right to its very core!

A. POOP TO THE RESCUE

We usually tend to think of **microbes**, or germs, as bad. They are, after all, the culprits that cause colds, the flu, tooth decay, and all kinds of other problems. But the truth is: we carry trillions of microbes around with us every single day. Many have no effect on us at all, plenty of others are actually good for us, and some are necessary for our survival.

You are made up of human cells, but there's so much more to you than that: you are an entire ecosystem! Believe it or not, your body

Microbes: any living thing that is too small to be seen with the naked eye, including bacteria, viruses, and some fungi and algae

contains about as many cells from things that aren't actually you as cells that are, maybe many more. They're a diverse group, too. You probably sustain more than 10,000 unique species of bacteria, viruses, and **protozoa**. And your specific personal collection, known as your microbiome, is completely different from that of the person sitting next to you.

Many of these microbes live in your gut. Some are "good bugs," which help you digest food, make vitamins, or keep you healthy simply by taking food and space away from the "bad bugs" that might make you sick. Researchers have found evidence suggesting a link between a person's microbiome and the risk of certain illnesses, including asthma, allergies, obesity, heart disease, multiple sclerosis, diabetes, depression, anxiety, schizophrenia, and more.

We can affect which microbes thrive in our guts (or not) by what we eat and the medications that we take (or don't). But sometimes that isn't enough. Occasionally, the bad bugs grow out of control or there aren't enough good ones to do their jobs. In those cases, more and more doctors are now using a procedure known as a fecal transplant. Yep, that's right: they take poop from a healthy person and put it inside the gut of a sick person! Pretty gross, right?

Maybe not. If you've been suffering from extreme and long-

Protozoa: tiny single-celled organisms

E. coli bacteria

term nausea, stomach pain, and diarrhea, and modern medicine has otherwise failed you, fecal transplantation could be just what you've been hoping for. First, it's been shown to be highly effective for certain **gastrointestinal** conditions. In many cases, patients recover

Gastrointestinal: having to do with the stomach and intestines

Stool: poop

completely within just a few days, and the results last longer than with other available treatments. Second, fecal transplants appear to be extremely safe, and without any unpleasant side effects. Third, it is a relatively inexpensive procedure.

So—poop aside, of course—what's not to love?

Some companies and nonprofit organizations, known as **stool** banks, are working to make this treatment more readily available for patients who could benefit from it. Potential donors are recruited and put through a rigorous testing and screening process. If the donors pass all the tests and appear to be

All in a day's work at the stool bank

perfectly healthy, the stool bank processes the donation, freezes it, and stores it. Then, doctors across the country can request a transplant whenever they have a patient who needs one.

So, the next time your stomach hurts or you're feeling like you might throw up . . . *no*, DO NOT try this at home, folks. That would be dangerous—and seriously disgusting! What were you thinking?

Strange Surgeries and Mysterious Medical Procedures

Which one of these is not a real treatment?

1. Hemicorporectomy: removal of the lower half of the body

2. Maggot therapy: using fly larvae to clean out dead tissue in a wound

3. Percutaneous ethanol injection of the liver: treating cancer with pure alcohol

4. Brackium emendo: hollowing out both ends of a broken bone to assist with proper realignment

5. Rhinoplasty: changing the shape and/or function of the nose

6. Full face transplant: yep, a new face

7. Gastropexy: attaching the stomach in place

8. Pinealectomy: removal of the pineal gland, which affects sleep patterns

9. Multiple subpial transection: cutting nerve fibers in the outer layers of the brain

10. Myringotomy: an incision in the eardrum

B. FRANKENSTEIN'S FIX

It might sound like something straight out of a horror novel: transplanting a human head from one body onto another. But for anyone facing a devastating illness that affects only their body—not their brain—it sounds more like a medical miracle. For 36-year-old Paul Horner, it turned out to be just the cure he had been so desperately hoping for.

Horner had suffered from a rare form of bone cancer for almost five years. As the disease progressed, it gradually rendered him unable to walk, drive, or even feed himself. He was told that his time was running out. But then, on February 17, 2015, something unbelievable happened. Doctors at the Charlotte Maxeke

It's complicated.

Johannesburg Academic Hospital in Parktown, South Africa, proposed a radical new surgery: to remove Horner's head and reattach it to a healthy donor body.

The donor was a young man who had been in a car accident and suffered irreversible brain damage. There had been no brain activity whatsoever for three years, and doctors were sure there was no hope for improvement. The body was perfectly healthy, however, and was being kept alive by machines. The donor's parents had decided it was time to remove the life-support systems, and they agreed to let Horner have their son's healthy body.

The surgery took more than 19 hours and relied on a team of specialists from a multitude of fields. They had to reattach blood vessels, nerves, and muscles. The windpipe and esophagus had to be rebuilt. Finally, a neurosurgeon had to reconnect the fragile but essential spinal cord.

The entire operation was led by Dr. Tom Downey. "It's

a massive breakthrough," he later told CNN. "We've proven that it can be done—we can give someone a brand-new body that is just as good, or better, than their previous one. The success of this operation leads to infinite possibilities."

It has taken months of recovery and physical therapy, but Horner can now do basic activities

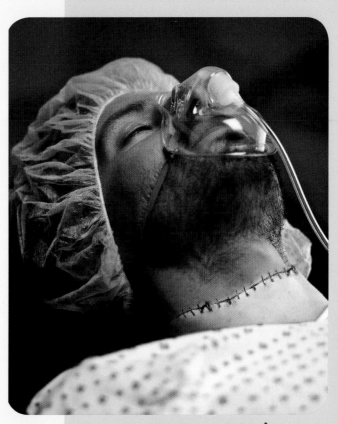

Paul Horner, right after surgery

like walk his dog, go up and down stairs, dress himself, and even shoot a basketball into a hoop. He may never be a star athlete, but it wasn't too long ago that all of this seemed like an impossible dream. "I was looking at the end of the road when the doctors offered me one last chance, to try this extremely risky procedure," he says. "They didn't know how well it would work, or if I'd even survive. But, really, what did I have to lose?"

In addition to a second chance at life, Horner has also been given the satisfaction of knowing that he has contributed to the advancement of science. His groundbreaking surgery helps pave the way for others, so that they can have a similar chance at a miraculous recovery. Plus, he's got a new career ahead of him. After achieving a certain level of fame for his unique situation, Horner is now able to earn a good living by appearing at live events and on television.

The hardest part? "Looking in the mirror," says Horner. "I still haven't gotten used to it."

Talk It Out

Modern medicine can treat many serious, life-threatening conditions with blood transfusions and organ or tissue transplants. Still, many people are uncomfortable with the idea of giving—or receiving—transplants. How do you feel about you or someone you love being an organ donor? Conversely, what conditions would make you agree to have someone else's blood, organs, or DNA transplanted in you?

C. PEE POWER!

One thing is for sure: what goes in must come out!

As long as people are alive, we'll be creating human waste in the form of urine (pee). But wouldn't it be cool if, instead of just flushing it all away, we could convert some of that waste into fuel? Talk about a sustainable and eco-friendly source of energy! Scientists from a variety of fields are working on accomplishing just that.

Professor Ioannis Ieropoulos, from the University of the West of England, is one of them. For 12 years, he and his team worked with a special type of battery called a microbial fuel cell (MFC). In MFCs, bacteria eat fuel and produce electricity. The trick was to find which fuel will produce the most energy. So Ieropoulos and his team fed MFCs all kinds of different fuels—wastewater, rotten fruit, prawn shells, dead insects, grass clippings, etc. Then they measured how much power each was able to generate.

Guess what came out number one? You got it—urine!

With urine as the fuel, the team was able to use MFCs

to generate enough electricity to power a cell phone for text messaging, Web browsing, and to make a brief phone call. The electricity output from MFCs is still relatively small, but over the next few years Ieropoulos and his team hope to develop and refine the process enough to fully charge a cell phone battery.

And that's not all. Ieropoulos wanted to see if they could have the same kind of success with wearable technology, so they created a pair of socks that were embedded with 24 miniaturized MFCs. The socks collected the wearer's urine through a soft tube in the heel. When the wearer walked, the movement of the feet could

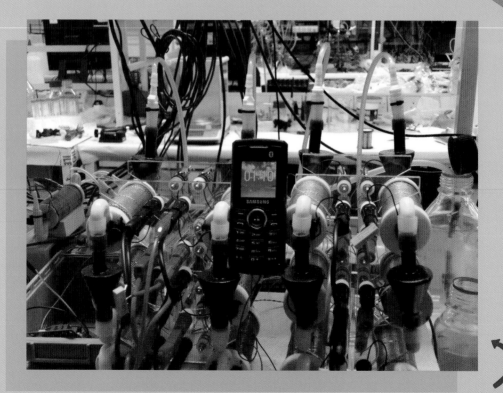

A cell phone in front of the urine-fueled MFCs used to charge it

pump the urine through more soft tubes over the MFCs in the socks. In lab tests, the sock MFCs were able to generate enough power to enable a wireless transmitter to send a signal to a nearby computer!

Okay, so urine-pumping, energy-generating, signal-sending socks probably aren't something you'd actually want to own just yet, but laboratory experiments like these could lead to some promising applications in the real world. Scientists are hoping to develop smart toilets for homes that could collect urine and use it to provide electricity for lighting, hot water, and bathroom appliances like razors and electric toothbrushes. And Ieropoulos is working with Oxfam, an international charity, to test and perfect a urinal that could be used to light restrooms. Those could be deployed in places like refugee camps, which often don't have any electricity and can be dangerous after dark.

New fashion trend? Um . . . no.

On an even grander scale, other scientists are trying to figure out how to use MFCs in city wastewater treatment plants. It takes a lot of energy to run these kinds of facilities today. Plus, most of the necessary energy currently comes from burning fossil fuels like coal, which causes pollution and contributes to global climate change. If we could successfully convert wastewater treatment plants to utilize MFCs, then we could eliminate many of the negative effects while actually generating electricity in the process. Now that's clean energy!

Although, you have to wonder: can we still call it "clean energy" . . . if it comes from pee?

Take Action

How should our leaders go about making policy decisions that affect both the rights of a single person and the overall health of the public? For example: Is it okay to ban smoking in public places? Should vaccinations be required? Should soft drinks or fatty foods be banned? Should children be required to have a fruit or vegetable with their school lunch? These are all topics that civic leaders have debated in recent years. Choose a rule that you'd like to see added or changed, and then write a statement expressing your opinion. If you'd like to take it a step further, collect signatures for a petition and send letters to those in charge. Maybe you can persuade the decision-makers to agree with you!

ONE THING YOU CAN *say about humanity: it brings no end of surprises! This selection includes helpful stuff you can do with poop; the world's first successful transplant of a human head; and some electrifying uses for pee. How quickly can you figure out the fake?*

A. A BRIEF HISTORY OF THE WORLD IN HICCUPS

It's happened to just about every person ever: You're going about your day, minding your own business. Then something happens, and suddenly—HIC! HIC! HIC!

Hello, hiccups.

A case of the hiccups might seem pretty unimportant: It's nothing but a series of quick little pop-squeaks in the throat that are more annoying than anything. You might even find it a little funny—especially if it's

 happening to someone else!

There's one guy, though, who definitely did *not* think hiccups were funny.

Charles Osborne was a farmer who lived in Iowa in 1922. One day, when he was working with his hogs, he picked one up—a huge pig, almost 350 pounds. And then, for no apparent reason, Osborne passed out. When he came to, Osborne wasn't in any pain. What he *was* in, however, was a full-blown case of the hiccups.

Lots, and lots, and lots of hiccups.

While scientists don't quite know why hiccups occur, they do know that they can be caused by many different

things—eating too much, drinking fizzy drinks too quickly, getting excited or stressed, or even just sucking in air the wrong way. Any of those things might cause an irritation in your diaphragm, the muscle at the bottom of your chest that puffs air into your lungs when you breathe.

It's likely that

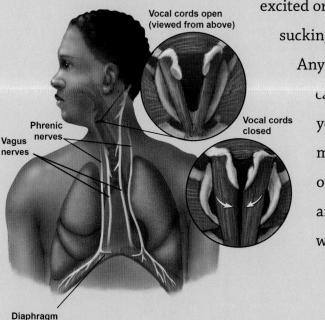

Vocal cords open
(viewed from above)

Vocal cords
closed

Phrenic
nerves

Vagus
nerves

Diaphragm

Charles Osborne wasn't worried about his hiccups at first. It's not uncommon for hiccups to last for many minutes, even up to several hours. Some people hiccup off and on for days. But Osborne's bout of hiccups began that day in 1922 and went on just a bit longer than that. He hiccupped from the beginning of World War II, in 1939, to its end, in 1945. He hiccupped from Elvis Presley's birth, in 1935, to Presley's death, in 1977. When Osborne started hiccupping, the very first televisions—showing black-and-white images only—were just being invented; when he died, nearly a quarter of all families in the United States had their own personal computer.

Aside from one 36-hour period, Osborne's hiccups never, ever let up.

Over the years, people told Osborne all the usual hiccup-attack remedies—from finger massage, to drinking water without taking a breath, to being scared witless—and he tried them all. Nothing worked. His hiccups paused only while he was asleep,

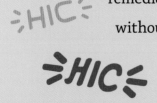

HIC but during the day Osborne eventually learned to swallow the telltale "hic" noise. He hiccupped once every three seconds for *68 years*, for a total of about 500 million hiccups over the course of his life!

It turned out that, on that day in 1922, a tiny, pin-sized blood vessel had burst in Osborne's brain, leading to the anomaly. Doctors all over the country examined him over the course of his lifetime, but no one was able to find him a cure.

Mysteriously, Osborne's hiccups stopped in 1990, almost a year before his death. It's hard to imagine how that must have felt! You have to wonder whether 96-year-old Charles Osborne basked in the blissful relief of his deliverance—or whether, sometimes, he missed the little pop-squeak that had been in the background for most of his adult life.

HIC

A Medley of Maladies

Only one of these isn't a real affliction. Can you guess which one it is?

1. Mad cow disease
2. Fragile X syndrome
3. Glanders
4. Fifth disease
5. Spattergroit
6. Cat scratch disease
7. Lockjaw
8. Monkeypox
9. Q fever
10. Hand, foot, and mouth disease

B. ME, MYSELF, AND . . . WHO?

In Greek mythology, a chimera is a monster made up of parts from more than one animal: a lion with the head of a goat and a snake for a tail, for instance. But in genetic terms, a chimera is an individual carrying two or more genetically distinct lines of cells. This means that a DNA test from one part of their body might not match one from a different part of their body.

Wait, two or more sets of DNA in the same person? Yep. Scientists used to think it was rare, but recent studies show that chimerism probably happens more often than we thought. In fact, *you* can become a chimera simply by being born! Twins often share a blood supply while in the womb, so

their cells can go back and forth and sometimes stick in the wrong body. Or, you might be your own twin! Sometimes, twin embryos fuse together and produce just one baby that has *both* sets of DNA. Cells also get transferred between a mother and her unborn child, so you probably have cells from your mom inside you. And your mom is almost certainly a chimera! She probably has some of *your* cells in her . . . and some from her mom, as well as some from any brothers or sisters you might have. Hey, that means *you* might have some cells from Grandma or an older sibling in you, too!

So, what does this all mean? Well, first of all, it can make things pretty confusing legally. One example is the case of Lydia Fairchild, who was tested along with her two children to prove who their father was. The tests confirmed the man was indeed their father— but that Fairchild couldn't possibly be their mother! She was taken to court and almost had her children taken away, but luckily her lawyer demanded she be tested further. At last, the mystery was solved: Fairchild was a chimera. What if chimerism showed up in a more serious legal scenario? Can you imagine a chimera leaving one set of DNA evidence at the scene of a crime (from blood, say), but police accidentally testing a different set of the criminal's DNA (maybe from the skin) as they investigated? They might mistakenly set the real criminal free, believing there was no way that person could possibly have committed the crime!

↑
← DNA strands

Chimerism has effects in the medical world, too. Studies have shown that some kinds of **autoimmune disorders** seem to be associated with chimerism, and chimera cells seem to be more common in children with diabetes and other pediatric diseases. Blood containing even a small fraction of an unexpected kind of cells has caused dramatic reactions when given to surgical patients. And what about transplants? Ask Karen Keegan from Boston. She'd already had one failed kidney transplant and was in need of another. She hoped that one of her three sons

Autoimmune disorders: conditions in which the body's immune system attacks itself

This person may have two genetically different cell lines determining eye color.

might be a match, but initial tests indicated that two of the three were not even her biological children! The doctors looked closer at Keegan's other tissues and eventually realized she was a chimera. How would they find a donor kidney for her? Which set of DNA should they try to match?

Chimerism obviously isn't all bad, since so many of us are likely to be chimeras and it doesn't usually cause us any problems. When it does, however, they can be extremely difficult to unravel and can challenge our very understanding of self. What makes you *you*, after all, if not your DNA?

Perhaps you can at least find some comfort in this: you're probably never truly alone.

A Bounty of Bizarre Body Parts

All of these are real terms used in human anatomy—except for one, of course!

1. Anatomical snuff box
2. Arcuate eminence
3. Falx cerebri
4. Ethmoid bulla
5. Infundibulum
6. Tuberius duct
7. Major calyx
8. Circle of Willis
9. Flexor digitorum profundus
10. Pons

I SPY WITH MY X-RAY EYES

If you could choose a superpower, what would it be? Invisibility, maybe? Or teleportation? If your choice is X-ray vision, you might be interested to know that a handful of people across the country would qualify as having legit superpowers.

And they're not at all happy about it.

It all started with a procedure called LASIK, which in 1999 became a government-approved method of correcting people's eyesight. Using a combination of laser technology and surgery, millions of people have now had

Cornea: clear window at the front of the eye

their **corneas** modified to give them perfect vision. No more glasses. No more contact lenses. What a dream!

For the vast majority of people, the story happily ends there.

For a very small percentage of

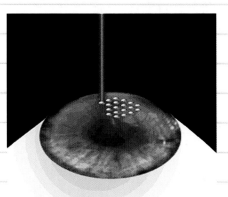

A laser preparing to cut a flap in the surface of a cornea

those patients, however, the dream rapidly turned into a nightmare. Take a patient known as Laura M., who underwent LASIK surgery in the spring of 2008. Not a candidate for the standard surgery, Laura elected for an experimental corneal onlay. The procedure appeared to go smoothly, and within several weeks of the successful surgery, Laura reported perfect vision with few side effects.

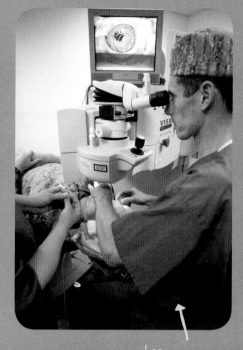

Laser eye surgery in progress

The only issue, she explained, involved her night vision, which occasionally seemed blurry and unfocused. These brief episodes quickly passed and Laura soon thought no more of them.

Until one night, on her way home from work, Laura looked at her fellow passersby and discovered . . . that she could see right through them! In a case of unintended side effects, the alteration of her eyes combined with low light levels pushed her vision to a shocking limit, giving her a form of X-ray vision. "The patient had an extraordinarily rare reaction to the procedure," concedes Bradley Standford, director of refractive surgery at the Carlson Vision Institute in Traverse City, Michigan. "Under certain extreme conditions, there were some disturbing side effects."

Disturbing, indeed. X-ray vision might sound like fun, but Laura and the few dozen patients who have had this side effect thrust upon them have found it to be anything but. "It turns everyone around you into a skeleton," one patient is recorded as saying. "Bones, jewelry, implants—it's all there for you to see. It's like living inside an X-ray machine."

Investigating doctors are quick to point out the extremely low rate of occurrence—about 0.0001%—making it so unlikely that it's hardly worth counting. (Tell that to Laura and the others!) Additionally, the X-ray vision only manifests at night, and usually in combination with fluorescent lighting. "It's an unfortunate situation," says Standford. "But when you weigh it against all the good LASIK has done, and continues to do—even for these patients—it really is a nonissue."

Whether it's a nonissue remains to be seen, as a pending lawsuit has yet to determine. And having now identified the cause of the anomaly, doctors insist that this type of side effect can no longer happen. But scientists hungry for a silver lining are digging into the research to see what, if anything, this could mean for the future of true, intentional X-ray vision.

Seeing skeletons around you? Not so cool. But being able to choose to see through certain things from time to time . . . now *that's* a superpower worth exploring.

Try This!

If modern medicine could enhance you in any way, what would you want to change about yourself? How would this "fix" make your life better? Would there be any drawbacks, challenges, or consequences? Write a story about what life would be like with your brand-new "superpower."

A PEEK ON THE *darker side raises all sorts of questions. Some of these include: Could someone really have the hiccups for 68 years? Is it possible for one person to have two separate DNA sequences? Could an operation give someone X-ray vision? Two of these are possible; one is not. And . . . go!*

A. THE CURE FOR THE COMMON WALLFLOWER

We all know someone who's a wallflower: Someone who sticks to the edges of the group, the class, or the party. Someone who's too shy to join in, but too timid to walk away. Yep, we all know a wallflower.

It's also likely that, at some time or another, most of us have probably *been* one.

But what if there was a way to get rid of that type of social paralysis altogether? We're not talking about pills or potions here, or any other kind of external or temporary behavior modifiers.

Instead, what if there was a way to actually cure a person's shyness?

This is the train of thought that is currently being pursued by Dr. Charlotte Sternfield, a cutting-edge **genetics** researcher with Nova

Genetics: how traits are passed from parent to child through generations

Gene therapy: replacing defective genes with healthy ones to cure genetic disorders

Genetics in Seattle, Washington. After decades of intensive study and experimentation, Sternfield and her team claim to have made significant strides in unlocking the genetic secrets behind sociability, offering a safe—and permanent—way to rewire the brain at its most basic level.

The result? An experimental **gene therapy** called CZ88. Or, informally, "Charisma."

Charisma was first made available for limited use in carefully monitored trials in March 2014, so the treatment is still extremely new, and experts caution against raising the public's expectations. But early trials were very positive, and Sternfield cites dozens of case studies of patients shedding their wallflower tendencies and embracing a newfound sense of confidence, poise, and, well . . . charisma.

"From outsider to life of the party," one source close to Sternfield quipped. The ultimate goal, Sternfield is quick to explain, is not popularity, but rather quality of life. Her aim is to reset the brain to its best capacity in social and interpersonal interactions, giving patients' self-confidence a boost and leading to greater success in life.

So far, by all accounts, CZ88 delivers.

But gene therapy expert

Jeanne Ryan

is not

convinced. "Anything that seems too good to be true usually *is*," says Ryan. "It's too early in the evolution of this treatment to say what the end result will be, as messing with the DNA for one trait could alter another trait or critical function. We need to view this whole process with extreme caution."

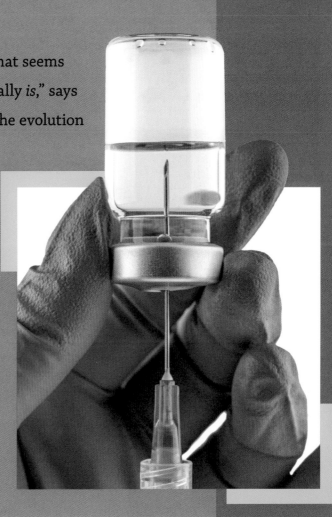

In fact, as early as mid-2016, mixed reports have been leaking out of Nova Genetics. Along with the rave reviews have come hints of darker side effects in some of those who have undergone the treatment. The delayed FDA approval—expected in early 2016 but not yet attained—hasn't helped things, either.

Still, if market response is any indicator, there are plenty of wallflowers more than willing to give CZ88 a shot, whatever its eventual outcome. "You're messing with the very building blocks of your body schematics," Ryan warns. "That's got to come with a price."

What that price will be, at this point at least, is anyone's guess.

Talk It Out

To protect people from ineffective treatments or potentially dangerous side effects, we have rules in place to determine when a particular medical intervention can be used to treat a specific disease or condition. Unfortunately, this also means that it can take a long time for new treatments to become available for patients who need them. How can we balance the need for public safety with the desire for access to the latest medical treatments? What kinds of guidelines should be in place to decide how a new treatment gets approved? What kinds of exceptions should be made, and when? Who should get to decide all of this: The patients? Their doctors? Other doctors? The corporations supplying the drugs or devices? The government?

B. THE BLOODY FOUNTAIN OF YOUTH

Aging seems to be inevitable: our bodies simply start to break down as we grow older. As a result, old age often brings various diseases and complications along with it: cancer, diabetes, **dementia**, heart problems, and slower healing, to name a few. Wouldn't it be nice if we could stay healthy, vibrant, and active for our entire lives, without ever being frail, sick, or forgetful? Well, we might find the answer . . . in our blood.

For centuries, physicians have tried to use blood from healthy people to cure the sick or to try to make old people feel young again. Some say that as early as 1492, Pope Innocent VIII's physicians attempted to revive him from a coma by giving him blood from three children. (Unfortunately, all

Dementia: a brain condition that makes it increasingly difficult to think, reason, and remember

Pope Innocent VIII

of them—the pope *and* all three boys—are said to have died in the process.) In the 1660s, London's Royal Society began experimenting with blood **transfusion**. With no understanding of blood types or what makes blood clot, however, experiments of that time were usually fatal as well. As a result, transfusion research came to a halt.

Transfusion: the transfer of blood from one body to another

Today, however, it's quite common for a person with a severe injury to receive a lifesaving blood transfusion. And there's a growing body of research indicating that blood could one day be used to achieve what so far has never been possible: to stop or even reverse the effects of the aging process.

In 2005, a researcher connected the circulatory systems of young mice (two to three months old)

with those of old mice (about two years old). He discovered injured muscle in the old mice healed faster when the blood of a young mouse was present in the old mouse's circulatory system. He also noticed that injured muscle in the young mice healed more slowly when they were receiving blood from an old mouse. Later, another group of scientists showed that the brains of old mice were able to produce more new neurons (nerve cells) after the old mice were given blood from young mice.

Does this mean kids like you will need to start volunteering to be blood donors? Will teenagers start selling their blood to the highest bidders? Will criminals start taking blood from young people . . . however they can get it? Let's hope it doesn't come to that! If scientists can identify which of the more than 700 components of young blood are responsible for its antiaging effects, or which ones in old blood might be causing the trouble in the first place, then perhaps they can find a treatment for aging that doesn't require draining youngsters of their precious blood.

Fortunately, recent studies in that area are showing promise. In 2013, researchers found that injections of a single protein from young blood could reduce the thickening of a mouse's heart muscle that typically occurs with old age. Later, they showed that the same protein, given all by itself, helps old mice recover from muscle injury almost as well as young mouse blood does. Another recent study identified higher levels of a different protein in the blood of old mice. When young mice received injections of only that specific protein, their ability to learn and remember things went down.

Results like these are very exciting. We could literally be on the brink of finally discovering the fountain of youth . . . and it may well be flowing red with blood. Let's just hope that blood doesn't have to come from young people like you!

Talk It Out

Is it ethical to experiment on animals? What are the reasons why scientists would want to? What dangers and problems might be associated with it? In your opinion, when might the potential benefits outweigh the concerns, and why? Who should get to decide?

C. REMOTE-CONTROLLED . . . BRAINS?!

So there you are: Sitting on the couch, watching TV. Your show's finished; you want to change the channel. What could be easier? You pick up the remote control. Click. Done. You don't even think twice, right?

But that's your TV. What if there was a button you could use to remote-control other things—animals, say. Or maybe even . . .

People?

These are the kinds of thoughts that must have gone through the mind of José Delgado, a professor of

Dr. Jose Delgado conducting his famous experiment

physiology at Yale University. He is best known for his research beginning in the 1950s into the area of mind control. Sound impossible? Think again. Delgado invented something called a stimoceiver, a tiny device that was built to— basically—mess with brain waves in order to change behavior. In a famous experiment, Delgado stepped into a ring with an enraged bull. The catch? The bull had a stimoceiver **implanted** in its brain.

Implanted: inserted through surgery

When Delgado pressed a button on his remote control, the bull stopped . . . midcharge! Delgado did similar work with cats and chimpanzees, and even moved on to experiment on some human patients.

Delgado's hope was to be able to curb and control brain

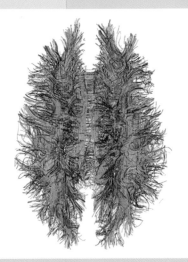

The wiring diagram of a brain!

disorders such as anxiety, schizophrenia, or depression. But the concept of mind control—in any form—is rife with controversy. Delgado's experiments were met with public outrage, and he gradually moved out of the public eye.

Still, the idea persisted, and Delgado's work was instrumental in a 2015 FDA-approved deep-brain stimulation treatment for Parkinson's disease. So, there are pros to this avenue of research and experimentation. And potential, too: In 2013, two University of Washington researchers designed an interface that hooked both of their brains up together (via the internet—what else?). By doing nothing more than thinking, the first researcher was able to move the second researcher's hand! Remotely!

Now that's some freaky stuff. And that also brings back all those ethical and

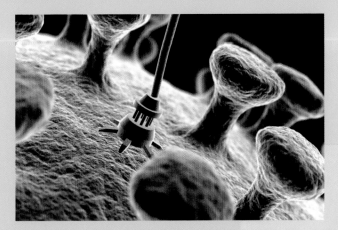

Close-up of stimoceiver in the brain

moral questions. What if someone *could* control your brain—through an implant or through a noninvasive internet link? What if that technology got into the wrong hands? What could possibly go wrong?

What, indeed.

Try This!

Some diseases and conditions are incurable—there is currently no medicine or treatment that can make them completely go away. If you could come up with a brand-new cure for any disease or condition, what would it be for? Why? How would it work? Would there be any potential side effects? Write and/or draw a picture about your choice.

WE'RE COMING TO THE end of this book, but there's still one set of mysteries left to solve. You've read about an experimental treatment that could cure shyness; the potential of young blood to remedy the diseases of old age; and a remote control that can be used on the human brain. Can you find the impostor hiding among the true stories?

RESEARCH GUIDE

We hope you haven't peeked at the answers already!

You haven't? Good! Why not see if you can figure out the fakes on your own, using the following research tips. And if you do already know the answers, well, here are some tricks you can use to guide you the *next* time you see something that makes you go, "Hmmm . . ."

In today's world, even professional researchers often start by searching the internet. In fact, we did nearly all of our research from the comfort of our homes using online resources! While that *is* convenient, there's a special challenge involved and good reason to be extra careful: on the web, it's hard to separate facts from fiction, and there are many people who'd love to fool you.

So, ready for the tips? Here we go.

Be engine-savvy: Internet search engines—such as Google—are essential, but should be used with care. They don't have a "truth filter," and they usually sort by what's most popular—so a well-known hoax might be the first thing on their list!

Our advice? Stick to links from a trusted source, such as a well-known university, a museum, an established newspaper or magazine, government agency, etc. Pay attention to when the information was posted and who the author is. And even when you do find what looks like a reliable source, try to verify your facts at two other reputable sources as well, to guarantee that it is widely considered true (and make sure they're not just referencing your first source!).

Be Wiki-wise: Wikipedia can be a great place to *start* your research on a given subject, but a true researcher would never stop there. Remember that Wikipedia articles can be edited by anyone at any time. So while most of the information you'll find there is likely true—you can never be sure.

Combat this by going straight to the source: Go to the end of an article and look for the References section. There, you will find links to other Web articles and/or citations for other resources like books, journals, or magazines. Make sure you explore those references, and even the references' references. Try to follow the trail until you get to a reliable source like the ones listed above.

Check the sources: Now that you know what makes a source more or less reliable, you can scan the sources listed for our stories (or any other questionable stories you happen to run across). First, if no sources are listed . . . be suspicious. Be very, very suspicious! If sources are listed, as they are in this book, take the time to scan through them to see if they look both reliable *and* relevant. Do the sources listed seem like they are probably trustworthy? Do they seem like they would be likely to validate the points that were included in the story?

Try to train yourself so that whenever you come across something surprising or hard to believe, your very first thought is, *Show me your source!* This simple trick will keep you from falling for most of what's out there.

Love your library: Another way we used the internet for our research was to access our local libraries. We couldn't write books like this if it weren't for libraries! There you can find online databases with all sorts of journal articles, old newspaper stories, magazine features, and more. A reference librarian even found us a paper copy of *Life* magazine from 1945 with original reporting (and photos) of one of the tales in this book!

The moral of the story: don't be afraid to ask a librarian for help with your research. That's what they're there for, and they truly are the experts.

Ask questions: Interviews with experts and witnesses are excellent sources as well. Can you talk to anyone who may have some background in a similar field to the story in question, such as a scientist or a doctor? See what they think of it! Know someone who lived through the time period in question? Find out if they remember anything about the event. (Yes, *you* can be an interviewer, just like we were. Most adults will be glad you asked!)

Use your noggin: Last but certainly not least, when you're judging what to believe or not believe—whether in the pages of this book or elsewhere—don't forget to employ your personal logic-o-meter. When you hear an unlikely-sounding story, think it through before doing anything else. How does it fit with what you know of how the world works? How does it settle into the boundaries of science, what you have read or seen on the news, and more? Learning to think critically will help you be a wise and careful judge of what you hear.

With these tips in mind, we hope you're able to figure out for yourself which stories in this book, and wherever else you find them, are true . . . and which ones are just pulling your leg.

If you're still stumped by any of ours, read on for the answers.

PART 1: PREPOSTEROUS PLANTS AND FUNGI-CRAZY, CREEPY, COOL

CHAPTER 1: CRAZY PLANTS

What a crazy hodgepodge of horticulture! But which one is the fake? If you guessed "Underground Miracle Root," then you are correct. This lie is based on some truths, though. The tuber fleeceflower (not its royal "cousin") is a real plant, which is grown in various provinces in China. The tuber fleeceflower is said to have health benefits, especially for the heart and liver. Those lumpy roots, however, do not bear any resemblance to humans. A quick online search will turn up quite a number of photos like the ones accompanying this story—but they're all fabrications. If you dig a little deeper, you can find photos of a variety of fruits and vegetables that have been mysteriously grown into all sorts of fascinating shapes—with the help of a plastic mold, which the fruit is placed into to shape it as it grows.

Plants: Fact or Fake?

The fake plant fact is "Spinach is not a vegetable. It is a fungus." But you already knew that, right?

CHAPTER 2: CREEPY PLANTS (AND FUNGI)

Frozen tundra hikers, rejoice: you do not have to fear the lurking slyrking. Yep, "Eyes Watching from the Darkness" is the fake in this section! Some light internet searching will turn up a creature of this type, but dig a little deeper and you will see that it is only found in the online role-playing game world of Santharia. Some things in this article are true, though: Svalbard is a real archipelago off the coast of Norway, and the shrinking glaciers are a real—and concerning—phenomenon (even without uncovering creepy moss stalkers), which is being studied by the Norwegian Polar Institute. And the photos in this story? One is fake, but as for the other, look up the awesomely named trash bugs (or lacewing larvae) for a special treat.

Real Plant Names

"Venomous tentacula" is not the name of a real plant. It may sound familiar, however, if you've read about it in a popular book of fiction.

CHAPTER 3: COOL PLANTS

As fabulous as it would be to have a homegrown night-light, the lie in this section is "Let There Be Flower Power!" This story has its seed in a real-life article that was published in the *German Gardener's News* in 1901, about a new variety of flower giving off enough light to read by. What day was it published? April Fool's Day, of course! Once again, some elements in this story are real. Carolus Linnaeus was a real naturalist, and really did design plans for an incredible flower clock in 1751. His clock, however, ended earlier in the evening. The western moonflower, as seen in the photo on page 35? It's a fake. False. Daan Roosegaarde? A real inventor, who is really doing some pioneering work with bioluminescence. As to what the end results will someday be— that's anybody's guess!

CHAPTER 4: SMALL ANIMALS

The animal kingdom is a wild place, isn't it? By now you might have figured out that, of the incredible creatures in this chapter, the fake is the star of "Puppy's Got a Brand-New Pal." Yep, we're sorry to say that the African threadsnake, of the symbiotic, ear-living wild dog affinity, is not real. (We kind of wish it was, to be honest!) Threadsnakes are real, though—the tiniest species of snake—and so are the endangered wild dogs of East Africa. The HERP Project is a real initiative, doing great work. You can look them up and see!

Great Groups!

We couldn't find reference to anyone ever actually calling a group of snakes a "hissing," though we imagine that is what one might sound like!

Crazy Creatures from under the Sea

Sadly, there is no creature known as the "layabout lobster." (But wouldn't it be cool if there were?)

CHAPTER 5: MEDIUM ANIMALS

The hoax of the Pacific Northwest tree octopus came to us almost fully formed, and as such might be a challenge even for savvy researchers to ferret out. A Google search will turn up a very professional-looking website created by Lyle Zapato and devoted to the Pacific Northwest tree octopus—but this website is, itself, an elaborate hoax. Octopods, we are kind of relieved to inform you, do not roost in trees. However, the National Oceanic and Atmospheric Administration recently discovered a brand-new octopod species living 14,000 feet under the ocean. So who knows what might be discovered in the months and years to come?

Animals: Fact or Fake?

It is not true that "horses often throw up their food hours after eating, just so they can eat it again." In fact, horses are unable to vomit at all, which can cause a whole bunch of very real problems!

CHAPTER 6: LARGE ANIMALS

Truth be told, we are not entirely ready to accept that creatures like Bigfoot, the Loch Ness Monster, chupacabras, and giant anacondas don't—and never did—exist. Still, "Megaconda—Myth No More" is an outright fake, since there is still no scientific proof of the existence of the giant snakes. Mike and Greg Warner probably really did travel to South America to try to find some, but they didn't bring back anything that would convince a biologist. What about the photos, you ask? Well, people seem to love making fake photos or videos of giant snakes, because this kind of internet hoax crops up fairly frequently. There was even a whole series of successful Hollywood movies about them! The megaconda might make for some popular fiction, but—thank goodness, right?—it is still just that.

Actual Dinosaur Names (or Are They?)

"Bookasaurus longuous" has never been used as the name of an actual dinosaur . . . at least not yet!

CHAPTER 7: HUMANS— YES!

We'll admit that—depending on your point of view—the idea of a head transplant might seem either pretty awesome . . . or downright disturbing. The story of the head transplant in "Frankenstein's Fix," however, is a fake. While doctors can perform many kinds of complex surgeries that do seem like modern miracles, they haven't yet figured out how to do everything that would be necessary to successfully transplant a human head—at least not when we were writing this book. The original story was, in fact, an internet hoax perpetrated by a well-known hoaxer. But that doesn't mean it won't someday be possible! Doctors *have* successfully transplanted the heads of animals, and Italian surgeon Sergio Canavero has been planning for a first attempt on a human to take place in China in 2017. He even has a patient who has already volunteered! So, who knows? Perhaps by the time you're reading this book, this one might be a little closer to true than we expected.

Strange Surgeries and Mysterious Medical Procedures

"Brackium emendo" is not a real medical treatment. It may, however, be a real magic spell. (We have never gone to wizarding school, so we can't be entirely sure.)

CHAPTER 8: HUMANS— NOOOO.

Ah, the power of wishful thinking at work! We regret to tell you that, as of this moment in history, X-ray vision is not a real thing, and "I Spy with My X-Ray Eyes" is the fake in this chapter. LASIK—a form of surgery to fix defective eyesight so corrective lenses are no longer needed—is a true and reliable procedure. However, at no time has LASIK ever given anyone X-ray vision. (We really are sorry. That prospect had potential! Even if seeing skeletons all around you sounds pretty darn spooky.)

A Medley of Maladies

Thankfully, "spattergroit" is a nasty skin infection that only appears in the pages of fictional tomes, not medical ones.

A Bounty of Bizarre Body Parts

"Tuberius duct" is not a real name of any part of the body. (But it could be, don't you think?)

CHAPTER 9: HUMANS— MAYBE?

For those of you who got excited at the prospect of a cure for shyness, science is not on your side. "The Cure for the Common Wallflower" is the made-up story in this section. While we do have more and more drugs available with which to treat mental-health conditions such as depression and social anxiety, no form of gene therapy has yet been approved for public use within the United States. Unfortunately, neither is CZ88. It is, however, the subject of a real novel for teens, the aptly titled *Charisma*, by Jeanne Ryan. And if you're still miffed that this is a hoax, then you may want to read that book, and you'll have an idea why—truly!—the world is better off without a lab-created charisma. Wallflowers, bloom on.

BIBLIOGRAPHY

PART 1: PREPOSTEROUS PLANTS AND FUNGI—CRAZY, CREEPY, COOL

CHAPTER 1: CRAZY PLANTS

Underground Miracle Root

Daily Mail. "Homer Really IS a Vegetable! Root Dug Up in China Looks Just like Simpson." Associated Newspapers. Last modified May 14, 2013. www.dailymail.co.uk/news/article-2324390/Root-dug-China-looks-just-like-Homer-Simpson.html.

Dietle, David. "10 Creepy Plants That Shouldn't Exist." Cracked.com. Last modified Jan. 27, 2011. www.cracked.com/article_18979_10-creepy-plants-that-shouldnt-exist_p2.html.

"Fleece Flower Root." ENaturalHealthCenter.com. Accessed Mar. 7, 2016. www.e2121.com/herb_db/viewherb.php3?viewid=536.

"Human-Shaped Fleeceflower Roots." Snopes.com. Accessed Feb. 7, 2016. http://message.snopes.com/showthread.php?t=70446.

"Radix Polygoni Multiflori." Shen-Nong. Accessed Feb. 7, 2016. www.shen-nong.com/eng/herbal/heshouwu.html.

Singh, Jagdev. "Chinese Fleece Flower." *Ayur Times*. Last modified Feb. 3, 2015. https://www.ayurtimes.com/chinese-fleece-flower/.

"Tapioca/Fleece-Flower Root!?" *FB Investigations* (blog). Jan. 3, 2014. http://fbinvestigations.blogspot.com/2014/01/this-post-is-going-around-as-tapioca.html.

Pandomonium

Curwood, Steve. "Living on Earth: The World's Largest Known Organism in Trouble." Living on Earth. Public Radio International. Transcript from radio, air date February 2013. http://loe.org/shows/segments.html?programID=13-P13-00005&segmentID=7.

Dewoody, Jennifer, Carol A. Rowe, Valerie D. Hipkins, and Karen E. Mock. "'Pando' Lives: Molecular Genetic Evidence of a Giant Aspen Clone in Central Utah." *Western North American Naturalist* 68, no. 4 (2008): 493–97. DOI 10.3398/1527-0904-68.4.493.

"Fishlake National Forest—Home." USDA Forest Service. Accessed Dec. 29, 2015. www.fs.usda.gov/detail/fishlake/home/?cid=STELPRDB5393641.

Grant, Michael C. "The Trembling Giant." *Discover*, Oct. 1993, 82–89. ProQuest Research Library (205981159).

Kisner, Jordan. "No Wonder It Quakes." *The American Scholar*, Spring 2015, 1617. ProQuest Research Library (1664940832).

Mitton, Jeffry B., and Michael C. Grant. "Genetic Variation and the Natural History of Quaking Aspen." *BioScience* 46, no. 1 (1996): 25–31. ProQuest Research Library (216462450).

Williams, Tyler. "Aspen in a Changing World." *American Forests*, Fall 2013, 2431. ProQuest Research Library (14446464940).

The Secret Lives of Plants

Das, Amitabha, Sook-Hee Lee, Tae Kyung Hyun, Seon-Won Kim, and Jae-Yean Kim. "Plant Volatiles as Method of Communication." *Plant Biotechnology Reports* 7, no. 1 (2012): 9–26. DOI 10.1007/s11816-012-0236-1.

Hughes, Sylvia. "Antelope Activate the Acacia's Alarm System." *New Scientist*, Sept. 29, 1990, 19. https://www.newscientist.com/article/mg12717361.200-antelope-activate-the-acacias-alarm-system.

Karban, Richard. *Plant Sensing and Communication.* Chicago: Univ. of Chicago Press, 2015.

Lewin, Sarah. "Mother Plants Tell Their Seeds When to Sprout." *Scientific American*, May 1, 2015. www.scientificamerican.com/article/mother-plants-tell-their-seeds-when-to-sprout/.

Pollan, Michael. "The Intelligent Plant." *New Yorker*, Dec. 23, 2013. www.newyorker.com/magazine/2013/12/23/the-intelligent-plant.

Suszkiw, Jan. "Plants Send SOS When Caterpillars Bite." *Agricultural Research* 46, no. 10 (1998): 20. ProQuest Research Library (208047366).

CHAPTER 2: CREEPY PLANTS (AND FUNGI)

The Flowery Smell of Death

Bradford, Alina. "Corpse Flower: Facts about the Smelly Plant." *LiveScience*. TechMediaNetworks. Last modified Aug. 21, 2015. www.livescience.com/51947-corpse-flower-facts-about-the-smelly-plant.html.

Hetter, Katia. "Alice the Corpse Flower Is Blooming in Chicago." CNN. Last modified Sept. 29, 2015. www.cnn.com/2015/09/29/travel/alice-corpse-flower-chicago-botanic-garden-bloom/.

Lijek, Suzanne (high school biology teacher). Phone interview with the author. Jan. 4, 2016.

Pappas, Stephanie. "Photos: Stinky 'Corpse Flower' Blooms." *LiveScience*. TechMediaNetworks. Last modified Aug. 20, 2015. www.livescience.com/51922-corpse-flower-photos.html.

Pettit, Anthonio. "Return of the Corpse Flower!" Friends of the Conservatory. Last modified Aug. 28, 2014. http://volunteerparkconservatory.org/return-of-the-corpse-flower/.

Shiff, Blair. "9 Things to Know about the Corpse Flower." 9News. Tegna. Last modified Aug. 19, 2015. http://legacy.9news.com/story/news/weird/2015/08/17/corpse-flower-fun-facts/31864935/.

"What Makes the Corpse Flower Stink So Bad?" *National Geographic*. Last modified Sept. 30, 2015. http://news.nationalgeographic.com/2015/09/150930-stinky-corpse-flower-chicago-botanic-garden-blooms/.

Eyes Watching from the Darkness

Holzman, Theodorus. "The Slyrking ("Walking Moss")." The Santharian Dream. Accessed Feb. 7, 2016. www.santharia.com/bestiary/slyrking_moss.htm.

"How Do Mushrooms Eat?" Yahoo! Answers. Accessed Feb. 7, 2016. https://answers.yahoo.com/question/index?qid=20081028155323AA8HDuZ.

"Svalbard's Glaciers Are Shrinking." Norwegian Polar Institute. Accessed Feb. 7, 2016. www.npolar.no/en/themes/glaciers/svalbard.html.

Winter, Lisa. "Moss Revived After 1500 Years of Permafrost." *IFLScience* (blog). Mar. 17, 2014. www.iflscience.com/plants-and-animals/moss-revived-after-1500-years-permafrost.

A Fungus among Us

Andersen, S. B., S. Gerritsma, K. M. Yusah, D. Mayntz, N. Hywel-Jones, J. Billen, D. P. Hughes, et al. "The Life of a Dead Ant: The Expression of an Adaptive Extended Phenotype." *American Naturalist* 174, no. 3 (2009): 424. http://ezproxy.kcls.org/docview/198756093?accountid=46.

de Bekker, Charissa, Lauren E. Quevillon, Philip B. Smith, Kimberly R. Fleming, Debashis Ghosh, Andrew D. Patterson, and David P. Hughes. "Species-Specific Ant Brain Manipulation by a Specialized Fungal Parasite." *BMC Evolutionary Biology* 14, no. 1 (2014): 166. DOI 10.1186/s12862-014-0166-3.

Loreto, Raquel G., Simon L. Elliot, Mayara L. R. Freitas, Thairine M. Pereira, and David P. Hughes. "Long-Term Disease Dynamics for a Specialized Parasite of Ant Societies: A Field Study." *PLoS ONE* 9, no. 8 (2014). DOI 10.1371/journal.pone.0103516.

"Parasite Causes Zombie Ants to Die in an Ideal Spot." *Science Scope* 33, no. 2 (2009): 8–9. ProQuest Research Library (225987991).

CHAPTER 3: COOL PLANTS

Watch Your Step!

Dundas, Deysia L. *Let's Go: Southeast Asia*. London: Macmillan, 2005.

Dyer, Bertie. "The Root Bridges of Cherrapunji." *Atlas Obscura* (blog). Slate. Last modified May 8, 2013. www.slate.com/blogs/atlas_obscura/2013/05/08/root_bridges_of_cherrapunji.html.

Hills, Suzannah. "What Would Health and Safety Say! The Amazing Indonesian Root Tree Bridge That Took 26 Years to Build . . . and If Local Folklore Is to Be Believed, Makes Dreams a Reality If You Swim beneath It." *Mail Online*. Associated Newspapers. May 13, 2013. www.dailymail.co.uk/news/article-2323364.

"Iya Valley Area." Japan National Tourism Organization. Accessed Jan. 3, 2016. www.jnto.go.jp/eng/location/regional/tokushima/iyakei.html.

Maier, Ulli. "Living Root Bridges of Cherrapunji." *Cookiesound Is Travelling* (blog). Jan. 3, 2016. www.cookiesound.com/2013/07/the-living-root-bridges-of-cherrapunji-in-megahalya-india/.

"Nature Treks and Walks." Cherrapunjee Holiday Resort. Accessed Jan. 4, 2016. www.cherrapunjee.com/activities/nature-treks-and-walks/.

Pulsipher, Lydia M., Alex Pulsipher, and Conrad M. Goodwin. *World Regional Geography: Global Patterns, Local Lives: Without Subregions*. New York: W.H. Freeman, 2008.

Stott, David, Vanessa Betts, and Victoria McCulloch. *India—The North: Forts, Palaces, the Himalaya Dream Trip*. Bath: Footprint, 2013.

Thuras, Dylan. "The Vine Bridges of Iya Valley." *Atlas Obscura* (blog). Slate. Accessed Jan. 3, 2016. www.atlasobscura.com/places/vine-bridges-japan.

Ver Berkmoes, Ryan. *Indonesia*. Footscray, Victoria: Lonely Planet, 2010.

Let There Be Flower Power!

Boese, Alex. "Sunflower Lamps." Museum of Hoaxes. Accessed Feb. 7, 2016. http://hoaxes.org/af_database/permalink/sunflower_lamps.

Callaway, Ewen. "Glowing Plants Spark Debate." Nature.com. Nature Publishing Group. Last modified June 4, 2013. www.nature.com/news/glowing-plants-spark-debate-1.13131.

"The Floral Clock." The All Watch. Accessed Feb. 7, 2016. http://theallwatch.com/the-floral-clock/.

"Getting Good Glow from Phosphorescent Products." Gardeners' Supply Company. Accessed Mar. 7, 2016. www.gardeners.com/how-to/glow-in-the-dark/8001.html.

Hamburger, Ellis. "A Natural Glow: These Plants Produce Their Own Light." *The Verge*. Vox Media. Last modified Mar. 14, 2014. www.theverge.com/2014/3/14/5504656/a-natural-glow-these-plants-produce-their-own-light-bioglow-daan-roosegarde.

Helmenstine, Anne Marie. "Make a Glowing Flower." About.com Education. Last modified Dec. 4, 2014. http://chemistry.about.com/od/glowingprojects/a/Glowing-Flower.htm.

Nass, Norbert, and Dierk Scheel. "Enhanced Luciferin Entry Causes Rapid Wound-Induced Light Emission in Plants Expressing High Levels of Luciferase." *Planta* 212, no. 2 (2001): 149–54. www.ncbi.nlm.nih.gov/pubmed/11216834.

"Plants That Give Light." *New York Times*. Apr. 22, 1883, 13. ProQuest Research Library (94094225).

Ragan, Sean Michael. "How-To: Fluorescent Flowers, the Easy Way." *Make: DIY Projects and Ideas for Makers*. Last modified Mar. 01, 2011. http://makezine.com/2011/03/01/how-to-fluorescent-flowers-the-easy-way/.

Shaffer, Leah. "For Sale: Plants That Glow in the Dark." *Discover*, Jan. 22, 2015. http://discovermagazine.com/2015/march/2-leafy-lighting.

Tortorello, Michael. "Five Minutes to Moonflower." *New York Times*. Jan. 28, 2015.
www.nytimes.com/2015/01/29/garden/planting-a-clock-that-tracks-hours-by-flowers
.html?_r=1.

The Sweet Truth

Anonymous. "Posters: T4 Nutrition and Management of Diseases." *Annals of Nutrition &
Metabolism* 63 (2013): 1133–395. DOI 10.1159/000354245.

Edible: An Illustrated Guide to the World's Food Plants. Washington, DC: National Geographic,
2008.

Endo, C., A. Hirata, A. Takami, I. Ashida, and Y. Miyaoka. "Effect of Miraculin on Sweet and
Sour Tastes Evoked by Mixed Acid Solutions." *Food and Nutrition Sciences* 6, no. 9 (2015):
757–64. DOI 10.4236/fns.2015.69078.

Inglett, G. E., B. Dowling, J. J. Albrecht, and F. A. Hoglan. "Taste Modifiers, Taste-Modifying
Properties of Miracle Fruit (*Synsepalum dulcificum*)." *Journal of Agricultural and Food
Chemistry* 13 (1965): 284–87. DOI 10.1021/jf60139a026.

Koizumi, Ayako. "Human Sweet Taste Receptor Mediates Acid-Induced Sweetness of Miraculin."
Proceedings of the National Academy of Sciences 108, no. 40 (2011): 16819–24. http://tealab
.ahau.edu.cn/docs/2014-05/20140524123934059828.pdf.

Lee, Roberta, and Michael J. Balick. "Without Sugar, Would the Holidays Be as Sweet? Exploring
Ethnobotanical Alternatives to Sucrose." *Alternative Therapies in Health and Medicine* 8,
no. 1 (2002): 98–99. www.nybg.org/files/scientists/mbalick/Without%20Sugar,%20
Would%20the%20Holidays%20be%20as%20Sweet.pdf.

Sun, H.-J., H. Kataoka, M. Yano, and H. Ezura. "Genetically Stable Expression of Functional
Miraculin, a New Type of Alternative Sweetener, in Transgenic Tomato Plants." *Plant
Biotechnology Journal* 5 (2007): 768–77. DOI 10.1111/j.1467-7652.2007.00283.x.

Zetter, Kim. "TED 2011: Can the Miracle Berry Prevent World Hunger?" Wired.com. Conde
Nast Digital. Last modified Mar. 2, 2011. www.wired.com/2011/03/miracle-berry/.

PART 2: ASTONISHING ANIMALS– SMALL, MEDIUM, LARGE

CHAPTER 4: SMALL ANIMALS

Puppy's Got a Brand-New Pal

Brahic, Catherine. "World's Smallest Snake Discovered." *New Scientist*, Aug. 3, 2008. www.newscientist.com/article/dn14453-worlds-smallest-snake-discovered/.

Carpenter, Jennifer. "World's Smallest Snake Discovered." BBC News. Aug. 3, 2008. news.bbc .co.uk/2/hi/science/nature/7537932.stm.

"HRE Study: Snakes and Their Habitats." HERP Project. Accessed Apr. 4, 2016. https:// theherpproject.uncg.edu/research/herpetology-studies/snakes/.

"Samburu Laikipia Wild Dog Project." Loisaba Conservancy. Accessed Apr. 4, 2016. www.loisaba.com/news_details.php?article=1237968213.

"World's Smallest Snake Found in Barbados." Pennsylvania State University. Last modified Aug. 3, 2008. http://news.psu.edu/story/184803/2008/08/03/worlds-smallest-snake-found-barbados.

The Tiny Guardians of Your Bookshelf

Buddle, Christopher. "Ten Facts about Pseudoscorpions." SciLogs.com. Last modified Apr. 1, 2014. www.scilogs.com/expiscor/ten-facts-about-pseudoscorpions/.

Cushing, Stanley Ellis, Anne C. and David J. Bromer. Curator of Rare Books and Manuscripts, Boston Athenaeum. Phone interview with the author. Jan. 8, 2016.

Hahn, Jeffrey, and Stephen Kells. "Psocids in Homes." University of Minnesota Extension. Accessed Apr. 7, 2016. www.extension.umn.edu/garden/insects/find/psocids/.

Jacobs, Steve. "Booklice." Department of Entomology. Penn State College of Agricultural Sciences. Last modified Dec. 1998. http://ento.psu.edu/extension/factsheets/booklice.

Jacobs, Steve. "Pseudoscorpions." Department of Entomology. Penn State College of Agricultural Sciences. Last modified July 2004. http://ento.psu.edu/extension/factsheets/pseudoscorpions.

Oswalt, Donny, Eric P. Benson, and Patricia A. Zungoli. "Booklice." College of Agriculture, Forestry and Life Sciences: Clemson University. Last modified Mar. 2004. www.clemson .edu/cafls/departments/esps/factsheets/household_structural/booklice_hs39.html.

"Pseudoscorpion (Order Pseudoscorpiones)." *Bug of the* Week (blog). University of Wisconsin— Milwaukee Field Station. Accessed Apr. 7, 2016. www4.uwm.edu/fieldstation/ naturalhistory/bugoftheweek/pseudoscorpion.cfm.

"Pseudoscorpions." Buglife—The Invertebrate Conservation Trust. Accessed Apr. 7, 2016. www.buglife.org.uk/bugs-and-habitats/pseudoscorpions.

Mighty Mollusks

Barber, A. H., D. Lu, and N. M. Pugno. "Extreme Strength Observed in Limpet Teeth." *Journal of the Royal Society Interface* 12, no. 105 (2015): 20141326. http://rsif.royalsocietypublishing .org/content/12/105/20141326.

Lu, D., and A. H. Barber. "Optimized Nanoscale Composite Behaviour in Limpet Teeth." *Journal of the Royal Society Interface* 9, no. 71 (2011): 1318–24. http://rsif.royalsocietypublishing .org/content/9/71/1318.

Martin, Ralph. "Modest Mollusk May Sport World's Strongest Material." *National Geographic*, Feb. 20, 2015. http://news.nationalgeographic.com/2015/02/150219-strongest-limpets- animals-science-technology-engineering-materials/.

"Scientists Find Strongest Natural Material." *UoP News*. University of Portsmouth. Last modified Feb. 18, 2015. www.port.ac.uk/uopnews/2015/02/18/scientists-find-strongest- natural-material/.

Viegas, Jennifer. "Nature's Strongest Teeth Belong to Aquatic Snails." *DNews*. Discovery Communications. Last modified Feb. 17, 2015. http://news.discovery.com/animals/ natures-strongest-teeth-belong-to-aquatic-snails-150217.htm.

CHAPTER 5: MEDIUM ANIMALS

Invasion of the Tree Octopods

"Conservapedia: Pacific Northwest Arboreal Octopus." *RationalWiki*. Last modified Jan. 28, 2016. http://rationalwiki.org/wiki/Conservapedia:Pacific_Northwest_Arboreal_Octopus.

Roush, Wade. "In Defense of the Endangered Tree Octopus, and Other Web Myths." *Xconomy RSS*. Last modified Aug. 8, 2008. www.xconomy.com/national/2008/08/08/

in-defense-of-the-endangered-tree-octopus-and-other-web-myths/.

Szydlowski, Mike. "Endangered: Pacific Northwest Tree Octopus Might Soon Disappear."
Columbia Daily Tribune, Aug. 26, 2015. www.columbiatribune.com/arts_life/family_life/
endangered-pacific-northwest-tree-octopus-might-soon-disappear/article_1c5d9e44-
f3c6-5326-be8e-d6047f3663a6.html.

Vendetti, Jann. "The Cephalopoda." University of California Museum of Paleontology. Accessed
Apr. 7, 2016. www.ucmp.berkeley.edu/taxa/inverts/mollusca/cephalopoda.php.

Zapato, Lyle. "Pacific Northwest Tree Octopus." Help Save the Pacific Northwest Tree Octopus
from Extinction! Zpi. Accessed Apr. 7, 2016. http://zapatopi.net/treeoctopus/.

The Extraordinary, Extra-Cranial Life of Mike

"Beheaded Chicken Lives Normally After Freak Decapitation by Ax." *Life*, Oct. 22, 1945, 53–54.

Cosgrove, Ben. "Life with Mike the Headless Chicken: Photos of a Famously Tough Fowl." *Time*,
May 30, 2013. http://time.com/3524433/life-with-mike-the-headless-chicken-photos-of-
a-famously-tough-fowl/.

Crew, Bec. "Meet Miracle Mike, the Colorado Chicken Who Lived for 18 Months without His
Head." *Scientific American Blog Network*. Sept. 26, 2014. http://blogs.scientificamerican
.com/running-ponies/meet-miracle-mike-the-chicken-who-lived-for-18-months-without-
his-head/.

Katzman, Rebecca. "Here's Why a Chicken Can Live without Its Head." *Modern Farmer*, Aug. 11,
2014. http://modernfarmer.com/2014/08/heres-chicken-can-live-without-head/.

Lambert, Kelly, and Craig H. Kinsley. *Clinical Neuroscience*. New York: Worth, 2005. https://
books.google.com/books?id=6OgdMLO0CdMC&lpg=PA84&dq=Mike%20the%20
Headless%20Chicken&pg=PA84#v=onepage&q=Mike%20the%20Headless%20
Chicken&f=false.

Lofholm, Nancy. "Sculpture Honors Mike the Headless Chicken." *Denver Post*, Mar. 31, 2000.
http://extras.denverpost.com/news/headless.htm.

"Mike the Headless Chicken Festival—Fruita, CO—June 3rd and 4th, 2016." Accessed Apr. 1,
2016. www.miketheheadlesschicken.org/mike.

Stokel-Walker, Chris. "The Chicken That Lived for 18 Months without a Head." BBC News. Last
modified Sept. 10, 2015. www.bbc.com/news/magazine-34198390.

Olmy Goodness, Tiny Dragons!

Arntzen, Jan Willem. "Proteus Anguinus." *IUCN Red List*. International Union for Conservation of Nature and Natural Resources. Accessed Mar. 7, 2016. www.iucnredlist.org/details/18377/0.

Bulog, Boris, and Arie Van Der Meijden. "*Proteus anguinus*." *AmphibiaWeb*. University of California. Last modified Dec. 26, 1999. http://amphibiaweb.org/species/4229.

Isalska, Anita. "10 Reasons to Visit Slovenia in 2015." CNN. Last modified Mar. 4, 2015. http://www.cnn.com/2015/03/03/travel/10-reasons-to-visit-slovenia-in-2015/.

Morton, Ella. "The Cave-Dwelling Baby Dragons of Slovenia." *Atlas Obscura* (blog). Slate. Accessed Feb. 7, 2016. http://www.slate.com/blogs/atlas_obscura/2014/05/28/olm_proteus_anguinus_also_known_as_baby_dragons_live_in_slovenia.html.

"Olm (*Proteus anguinus*)." *EDGE of Existence*. Zoological Society of London. Accessed Mar. 7, 2016. www.edgeofexistence.org/amphibians/species_info.php?id=563.

"Vivarium Proteus." *Postojna Cave*. Postojnska Jama. Accessed Mar. 7, 2016. www.postojnska-jama.eu/en/come-and-visit-us/vivarium-proteus/.

CHAPTER 6: LARGE ANIMALS

Discovering Prehistoric Bambi

Burnham, David A., Preparator, Biodiversity Institute & Natural History Museum at the University of Kansas. Email with the author. Feb. 1, 2016.

Devlin, Sherry. "Dinosaur Discovery." *Missoulian*, Jan. 22, 2000. http://missoulian.com/uncategorized/dinosaur-discovery/article_a8083c89-257b-5a4b-9535-6c14b50fc4a0.html.

Devlin, Sherry. "Stevensville Family Unearths Dinosaur." *Helena Independent Record*, Mar. 18, 2000. http://helenair.com/lifestyles/recreation/stevensville-family-unearths-dinosaur/article_f3088fc4-719e-5fae-b519-06f6df703a37.html.

"A Dinosaur Named Bambi." *Factmonster—Time for Kids Magazine*, Mar. 24, 2000. www.factmonster.com/tfk/magazines/story/0,6277,48969,00.html.

Dorfman, Andrea. "A Dino Named Bambi." *Time*, Mar. 19, 2000. http://content.time.com/time/magazine/article/0,9171,41191,00.html.

Holden, Constance. "Another Birdlike Dino Unveiled." *Science*. American Association for the

Advancement of Science. Mar. 17, 2000. www.sciencemag.org/news/2000/03/another-birdlike-dino-unveiled.

Holden, C. "Florida Meeting Shows Perils, Promise of Dealing for Dinos." *Science* 288, no. 5464 (2000), 238–39. ProQuest Research Library (213572985).

"A New Species." American Museum of Natural History. Accessed Apr. 4, 2016. www.amnh.org/exhibitions/dinosaurs-ancient-fossils-new-discoveries/introduction/a-new-species.

Paul, Gregory S. *The Princeton Field Guide to Dinosaurs.* Princeton, NJ: Princeton Univ. Press, 2010. https://books.google.com/books?id=wdKBfB2k9asC&lpg=PA135&dq=bambiraptor%20feinbergi&pg=PA135#v=onepage&q=bambiraptor%20feinbergi&f=false.

Megaconda—Myth No More

"Biggest Snake: Giant Anaconda." Extreme Science. Accessed Feb. 5, 2016. www.extremescience.com/biggest-snake.htm.

"Herpetologist: Jesus Rivas." Extreme Science. Accessed Feb. 5, 2016. www.extremescience.com/jesus-rivas.htm.

Milord, Luckele. "*Eunectes murinus* (Anaconda, Green Anaconda)." *Animal Diversity Web.* University of Michigan Museum of Zoology. Accessed Feb. 5, 2016. http://animaldiversity.org/site/accounts/information/Eunectes_murinus.html.

Rivas, Jesus. "Jesus Rivas's Home Page." Accessed Feb. 5, 2016. www.anacondas.org.

Warner, Mike. "Big Snakes." Accessed Feb. 28, 2016. www.bigsnakes.info.

White, Laurence. "What's Stirring in the Jungle?" *Belfast Telegraph.* Last modified Aug. 6, 2009. www.belfasttelegraph.co.uk/opinion/columnists/archive/laurence-white/whats-stirring-in-the-jungle-28482403.html.

Gelatinous Curtain of Death

Dunn, Casey. "Siphonophores." Accessed Jan. 28, 2016. www.siphonophores.org.

Dunn, Casey W., Philip R. Pugh, and Steven H. D. Haddock. "Molecular Phylogenetics of the Siphonophora (Cnidaria), with Implications for the Evolution of Functional Specialization." *Systematic Biology* 54, no. 6 (2005): 916–35. DOI 10.1080/10635150500354837.

"Giant Siphonophore." Deep Sea, Invertebrates, *Praya* Sp at the Monterey Bay Aquarium. Accessed Feb. 2, 2016. www.montereybayaquarium.org/animal-guide/invertebrates/giant-siphonophore.

Hunter, Carol. "The Deep Next Door." *Terrain Magazine* (blog). Ecology Center. Last modified

Aug. 15, 2002. http://ecologycenter.org/terrainmagazine/fall-2002/the-deep-next-door/.

Nadis, Steve. "Creatures of the Twilight Zone." *Popular Science* 253, no. 3 (Sept. 1998): 50–55. ProQuest Research Library (222940254).

Raskoff, Kevin A., et al. "Collection and Culture Techniques for Gelatinous Zooplankton." *Biological Bulletin* 204, no. 1 (2003): 68–80. www.mpcfaculty.net/kevin_raskoff/raskoffCulture.pdf.

Tangley, Laura. "Mysteries of the Twilight Zone—Once Dismissed as a Biological Wasteland, the Deep Sea Teems with Surprising Life Forms, Most of Them Unknown to Science." *National Wildlife*, Oct.–Nov. 2001. www.nwf.org/News-and-Magazines/National-Wildlife/Animals/Archives/2001/Mysteries-of-the-Twilight-Zone.aspx.

Wrobel, Dave. "Siphonophores." Accessed Feb. 2, 2016. http://jellieszone.com/siphonophores/.

PART 3: HOW ABOUT HUMANS—YES! NOOOO. MAYBE?

CHAPTER 7: HUMANS—YES!

Poop to the Rescue

Bull, Matthew J., and Nigel T. Plummer. "Part 1: The Human Gut Microbiome in Health and Disease." *Integrative Medicine* 13, no. 6 (2015): 17–22. www.ncbi.nlm.nih.gov/pmc/articles/PMC4566439/.

Coburn, Bryan, and David S. Guttman. "The Human Microbiome." *Canadian Medical Association Journal* 187, no. 11 (2015): 825. ProQuest Research Library (1704725688).

"Home." OpenBiome. Last modified May 8, 2016. www.openbiome.org/

Khanna, Sahil, and Pritish K. Tosh. "A Clinician's Primer on the Role of the Microbiome in Human Health and Disease." *Mayo Clinic Proceedings* 89, no. 1 (2014): 107–14. ProQuest Research Library (1477197652).

Marchione, Marilynn. "Just Say 'Ick': Poop Pill Can Cure Infection; Canadian Researchers Clean Up the 'Fecal Transplant' Process for Treating Patients after Antibiotics Fail to Help." *Los Angeles Times*, Oct. 6, 2013. ProQuest Research Library (1439573412).

"Me, Myself, Us; the Human Microbiome." *Economist*, Aug. 18, 2012, 69. www.economist.com/node/21560523.

Pollan, Michael. "Some of My Best Friends Are Germs." *New York Times*, May 18, 2013. www.nytimes.com/2013/05/19/magazine/say-hello-to-the-100-trillion-bacteria-that-make-up-your-microbiome.html.

Frankenstein's Fix

Lamont, Tom. "'I'll Do the First Human Head Transplant.'" *The Guardian*, Oct. 3, 2015. www.theguardian.com/science/2015/oct/03/will-first-human-head-transplant-happen-in-2017.

Rubics, Darius. "World's First Head Transplant a Success After Nineteen Hour Operation." *News Examiner*, Apr. 9, 2015. http://newsexaminer.net/health/worlds-first-head-transplant-a-success/.

Wong, Sam. "Head Transplant Carried Out on Monkey, Claims Maverick Surgeon." *New Scientist*, Jan. 19, 2016. www.newscientist.com/article/2073923-head-transplant-carried-out-on-monkey-claims-maverick-surgeon/.

Pee Power!

Ieropoulos, Ioannis A., Pablo Ledezma, Andrew Stinchcombe, George Papaharalabos, Chris Melhuish, and John Greenman. "Waste to Real Energy: The First MFC Powered Mobile Phone." *Physical Chemistry Chemical Physics* 15, no. 37 (2013): 15312. http://pubs.rsc.org/en/content/articlehtml/2013/cp/c3cp52889h.

Institute of Physics. "Wearable Energy Generator Uses Urine to Power Wireless Transmitter." *ScienceDaily*. Last modified Dec. 11, 2015. www.sciencedaily.com/releases/2015/12/151211130103.htm.

Jezard, Adam. "Eco Project Takes Urine Seriously." *Financial Times*, Nov. 18, 2014. www.ft.com/cms/s/2/d704de86-6695-11e4-9c0c-00144feabdc0.html.

Knapton, Sarah. "Wee-Fi: Urine-Powered Socks Can Send Message in Emergency." *Telegraph*, Dec. 11, 2015. www.telegraph.co.uk/news/science/science-news/12046628/Wee-fi-urine-powered-socks-can-send-message-in-emergency.html.

Li, Wen-Wei, Han-Qing Yu, and Zhen He. "Towards Sustainable Wastewater Treatment by Using Microbial Fuel Cells-Centered Technologies." *Energy & Environmental Science* 7, no. 3 (2013): 911–24. http://pubs.rsc.org/en/content/articlehtml/2014/ee/c3ee43106a.

"Mobile Phone Runs on Urine Power." Bristol Robotics Laboratory. University of the West of England and the University of Bristol. Last modified Dec. 3, 2015. www.brl.ac.uk/brlinthenews/urinepower.aspx.

"'Pee-Power' to Light Camps in Disaster Zones." Oxfam International. Last modified Mar. 5, 2015. www.oxfam.org/en/pressroom/pressreleases/2015-03-05/pee-power-light-camps-disaster-zones.

CHAPTER 8: HUMANS—NOOOO.

A Brief History of the World in Hiccups

Crockett, Zachary. "The Man Who Continuously Hiccuped for 68 Years." *Priceonomics*. June 19, 2015. http://priceonomics.com/the-man-who-hiccuped-for-68-years/.

"Hiccups." Mayo Clinic. Last modified Aug. 6, 2015. www.mayoclinic.org/diseases-conditions/hiccups/basics/causes/con-20031471.

James, Susan Donaldson. "Tumor-Induced Hiccups Rob Man of Job, Music." ABC News Network. Last modified Jan. 13, 2010. http://abcnews.go.com/Health/british-man-hiccups-diagnosed-brain-tumor-doctors-baffled/story?id=9544425.

"Longest Attack of Hiccups." BBC News. Accessed Mar. 31, 2016. http://news.bbc.co.uk/2/shared/spl/hi/pop_ups/05/health_guinness_medical_record_breakers/html/2.stm.

Singer, Connie. "A Cure for Hiccups? Retired Farmer Charles Osborne Isn't Holding His Breath—He's Had Them for 60 Years." *People*, Mar. 29, 1982. www.people.com/people/archive/article/0,,20081781,00.html.

Van Buren, Abigail. "Charlie Needs Your Hiccup Cure." *Gainesville Sun*, Sept. 16, 1987. https://news.google.com/newspapers?id=ez5WAAAAIBAJ&sjid=BuoDAAAAIBAJ&pg=6526%2C78674.

Me, Myself, and . . . Who?

Doucleff, Michaeleen. "Fetal Cells May Protect Mom from Disease Long After the Baby's Born." NPR recording, 4:20. Oct. 26, 2015. www.npr.org/sections/health-shots/2015/10/26/449966350.

Ford, Andrea. "Maternal-Fetal 'Chimera' Cells: What Do They Actually Do?" *Scope Blog*. Stanford Medicine. Sept. 9, 2015. http://scopeblog.stanford.edu/2015/09/09/maternal-fetal-chimera-cells-what-do-they-actually-do/.

Gadi, Vijayakrishna K. "Fetal Microchimerism in Breast from Women with and without Breast Cancer." *Breast Cancer Research and Treatment* 121, no. 1 (2010): 241–44. ProQuest Research Library (193485640).

Giorgi, Elena E. "From Many, One." *Scientist*. LabX Media Group. Last modified Apr. 1, 2015.
www.the-scientist.com/?articles.view/articleNo/42476/title/From-Many--One/.

Nelson, J. L. "The Otherness of Self: Microchimerism in Health and Disease." *Trends in Immunology* 33, no. 8 (2012): 421–27. http://www.ncbi.nlm.nih.gov/pmc/articles/PMC3516290/.

Robson, David. "Is Another Human Living inside You?" BBC. Last modified Sept. 18, 2015.
www.bbc.com/future/story/20150917-is-another-human-living-inside-you.

Thompson, Emma E., et al. "Maternal Microchimerism Protects Against the Development of Asthma." *Journal of Allergy and Clinical Immunology* 132, no. 1 (2013): 39–44. DOI 10.1016/j.jaci.2012.12.1575.

Wolinsky, Howard. "A Mythical Beast. Increased Attention Highlights the Hidden Wonders of Chimeras." EMBO Reports. U.S. National Library of Medicine. Last modified Mar. 2007.
www.ncbi.nlm.nih.gov/pmc/articles/PMC1808039/.

Zimmer, Carl. "DNA Double Take." *New York Times*, Sept. 16, 2013. www.nytimes.com/2013/09/17/science/dna-double-take.html?_r=0.

I Spy with My X-Ray Eyes

Cooper, Tarquin. "'Laser Eye Surgery Has Given Me Superman Vision.'" *Telegraph*, Mar. 8, 2010.
www.telegraph.co.uk/news/health/7374893/Laser-eye-surgery-has-given-me-Superman-vision.html.

"The History of LASIK Surgery." The LASIK Vision Institute. Last modified Aug. 13, 2013.
www.lasikvisioninstitute.com/the-history-of-lasik-surgery/.

Horn, Marion. "X-ray Vision Surgery." *Fraunhofer Magazine*, 2005, 26–27. www.archiv
.fraunhofer.de/archiv/magazin04-08/fhg/Images/magazine1-2005-26f_tcm6-14058.pdf.

"LASIK Risks, Complications, Side Effects, Problems." LasikComplications.com. Accessed Mar. 30, 2016. http://lasikcomplications.com/risks.htm.

McKenna, Phil. "X-Ray Vision Is Here." PBS. Last modified Sept. 24, 2014. www.pbs.org/wgbh/nova/next/military/x-ray-vision/.

"MIT Researchers Invent Wireless 'X-Ray Vision' with New Project, Emerald." CBSNews. Last modified Dec. 9, 2015. www.cbsnews.com/news/mit-researchers-invent-wireless-x-ray-vision-project-emerald/.

Thompson, Vance. "Corneal Inlays and Corneal Onlays." *All About Vision*. Access Media Group. Last modified Dec. 2015. www.allaboutvision.com/visionsurgery/corneal-inlays-onlays.htm.

CHAPTER 9: HUMANS—MAYBE?

The Cure for the Common Wallflower

"Gene Therapy Successes." University of Utah. Accessed Apr. 4, 2016. http://learn.genetics.utah .edu/content/genetherapy/gtsuccess/.

"Jeanne Ryan—Charisma." Gorge News Center. Last modified May 27, 2015. http:// gorgenewscenter.com/jeanne-ryan-charisma/.

Lickerman, Alex. "How to Overcome Shyness." *Psychology Today*, June 19, 2011. www .psychologytoday.com/blog/happiness-in-world/201106/how-overcome-shyness.

Lydiard, R. Bruce, and Julio Bobes. "Therapeutic Advances: Paroxetine for the Treatment of Social Anxiety Disorder." *Depression and Anxiety* 11, no. 3 (2000): 99–104. www.ncbi.nlm .nih.gov/pubmed/10875050.

Ryan, Jeanne. *Charisma*. New York: Penguin, 2015.

Stein, Murray B., Michael R. Liebowitz, R. Bruce Lydiard, Cornelius D. Pitts, William Bushnell, and Ivan Gergel. "Paroxetine Treatment of Generalized Social Phobia (Social Anxiety Disorder)." *JAMA* 280, no. 8 (1998): 708. http://jama.jamanetwork.com/article .aspx?articleid=187901.

The Bloody Fountain of Youth

Conboy, Irina M., Michael J. Conboy, Amy J. Wagers, Eric R. Girma, Irving L. Weissman, and Thomas A. Rando. "Rejuvenation of Aged Progenitor Cells by Exposure to a Young Systemic Environment." *Nature* 433, no. 7027 (2005): 760–64. ProQuest Research Library (204596680).

Paul, Steven M., and Kiran Reddy. "Young Blood Rejuvenates Old Brains." *Nature Medicine* 20, no. 6 (2014): 582–83. https://web.stanford.edu/group/twclab/cgi-bin/images/TWClab/ publications/2014_villeda_natmed_newsviews.pdf.

Phimister, Elizabeth G., and Alessandro Laviano. "Young Blood." *New England Journal of Medicine* 371, no. 6 (2014): 573–75. ProQuest Research Library (1551986349).

Sample, Ian. "Can We Reverse the Ageing Process by Putting Young Blood into Older People?" *Guardian*, Aug. 4, 2015. www.theguardian.com/science/2015/aug/04/can-we-reverse- ageing-process-young-blood-older-people.

Scott, Christopher Thomas, and Laura Defrancesco. "Selling Long Life." *Nature Biotechnology* 33, no. 1 (2015): 31–40. ProQuest Research Library (1644157714).

Scudellari, Megan. "Blood to Blood." *Nature* 517, no. 7535 (2015): 426–29. ProQuest Research Library (1649791808).

Secko, David. "Young Blood Heals Old Muscles." *Canadian Medical Association Journal* 172, no. 7 (2005): 869. www.cmaj.ca/content/172/7/869.full.

Villeda, Saul A., et al. "Young Blood Reverses Age-Related Impairments in Cognitive Function and Synaptic Plasticity in Mice." *Nature Medicine* 20, no. 6 (2014): 659–63. ProQuest Research Library (1532983179).

Remote-Controlled . . . Brains?!

Anthony, Sebastian. "First Human Brain-to-Brain Interface Allows Remote Control over the Internet, Telepathy Coming Soon." ExtremeTech. Ziff Davis. Last modified Aug. 28, 2013. www.extremetech.com/extreme/165081-first-human-brain-to-brain-interface-allows-remote-control-over-the-internet-telepathy-coming-soon.

Delgado, J. M. R. "Instrumentation, Working Hypotheses, and Clinical Aspects of Neurostimulation." *Stereotactic and Functional Neurosurgery* 40, no. 2–4 (1977): 88–110. www.karger.com/Article/Abstract/102436#.

"FDA Approves Brain Implant to Help Reduce Parkinson's Disease and Essential Tremor Symptoms." U.S. Food and Drug Administration. Last modified June 22, 2015. www.fda.gov/NewsEvents/Newsroom/PressAnnouncements/ucm451152.htm.

Horgan, John. "The Forgotten Era of Brainchips." *Scientific American*, Oct. 2005, 66–73. www.wireheading.com/delgado/brainchips.pdf.

Horgan, John. "The Myth of Mind Control." *Discover*, Oct. 2004. https://discovermagazine.com/2004/oct/cover/.

"José Delgado, Implants, and Electromagnetic Mind Control." YouTube video, 1:07, from a 1985 CNN Special. Posted by Kevin Crosby Jan. 2, 2013. www.youtube.com/watch?v=23pXqY3X6c8.

Ma, Michelle. "UW Study Shows Direct Brain Interface between Humans." *UW Today*. University of Washington. Last modified Nov. 5, 2014. www.washington.edu/news/2014/11/05/uw-study-shows-direct-brain-interface-between-humans/.

Scarf, Maggie. "Brain Researcher Jose Delgado Asks—'What Kind of Humans Would We Like to Construct?'" *New York Times*, Nov. 15, 1970. ProQuest Research Library (118906529).

"Transcranial Magnetic Stimulation." Mayo Foundation for Medical Education and Research. Last modified Dec. 3, 2015. www.mayoclinic.org/tests-procedures/transcranial-magnetic-stimulation/home/ovc-20163795.

Veronese, Keith. "The Scientist Who Controlled People with Brain Implants." *io9* (blog). Gizmodo. Dec. 28, 2011. http://io9.gizmodo.com/5871598.

Zheng, Henry. "The Brain-Machine Connection: Humans and Computers in the 21st Century." *Yale Scientific Magazine*, Feb. 13, 2011. www.yalescientific.org/2011/02/the-brain-machine-connection-humans-and-computers-in-the-21st-century/.

PHOTOGRAPH CREDITS

The authors would like to thank the following for granting permission to reproduce the images used in this book:

page 1 © SnowWhiteimages/Shutterstock
page 2 © Xiao caoming - Imaginechina/AP Photo
page 3 © dovla982/Shutterstock
page 4 © Xiao caoming - Imaginechina/AP Photo
page 5 © aphotostory/Shutterstock
page 6 © the_lazy_pigeon/Shutterstock
page 7 Ken Lund/Flickr
page 8 Don Breneman, University of Minnesota Extension
page 9 Mark Muir/USDA Forest Service
page 11 Frédéric Salein/Wikimedia Commons
page 12 USDA.gov/Flickr
page 13 Scott Bauer/USDA
page 16 U.S. Botanic Garden
page 17 © Tony Larkin/REX/Shutterstock
page 20 Per Harald Olsen/Wikimedia Commons
page 21 © Sammy Yuen
page 22 Sanja565658/Wikimedia Commons
page 25 © Alex Wild/alexanderwild.com
page 26 David P. Hughes, Maj-Britt Pontoppidan/Wikimedia Commons
page 28 © Intrepix/Shutterstock
page 29 ume-y/Wikimedia Commons
page 30–31 © Michal Knitl/Shutterstock
page 33 Hendrik Hollander/Wikimedia Commons
page 34 Greg O'Beirne/Wikimedia Commons
page 35 © Sammy Yuen
page 36 Epibase/Wikimedia Commons
page 38 © Gaulois_s/Shutterstock
page 39 Miracle Fruit Farm/Wikimedia Commons
page 41 © Joe Fornabaio/The New York Times/Redux; (background) Forest & Kim Starr/Wikimedia Commons
page 42 © leungchopan/Shutterstock
page 44 (photo) Blair Hedges, Penn State/Wikimedia Commons; (diagram) Rlawson/en.wikibooks
page 45 Derek Keats/Flickr
page 46 © Sammy Yuen
page 48 JN~commonswiki/Wikimedia Commons

page 49 Juan Antonio F. Segal/Flickr

page 51 Lawrie Cate/Flickr

page 52 University of Portsmouth

page 53 © Jason Smalley Photography/Alamy Stock Photo

page 57 © (eagle) Carl Chapman/Wikimedia Commons; (octopus) Laika ac/Flickr; (trees) HaSee/German Wikipedia; (composite) Lelynn Ruggles

page 58 zapatopi.net/treeoctopus

page 61 © Bob Landry/The LIFE Picture Collection/Getty Images

page 62 City of Fruita

page 64 © Nature Picture Library/Alamy Stock Photo

page 65 Nacionalni park Una66/Wikimedia Commons

page 66 © Ladi Kirn/Alamy Stock Photo

page 67 Maull & Fox/Wikimedia Commons; Unknown/Wikimedia Commons

page 69 © Olinchuk/Shutterstock

page 70 Sergio Kaminski/Wikimedia Commons

page 71 © Stocktrek Images, Inc./Alamy Stock Photo

page 72 Thesupermat/Wikimedia Commons

page 75 Daniel Candido/Wikimedia Commons

page 76 © Sammy Yuen

page 77 © Sammy Yuen

page 79 © S. Haddock/MBARI

page 80 © S. Haddock/MBARI

page 82 Monterrey Bay Aquarium Research Institute (MBARI)

page 84 © dencg/Shutterstock

page 86 National Institute of Allergy and Infectious Diseases (NIAID), NIH/Wikimedia Commons

page 87 © Erik Jacobs/The New York Times/Redux Pictures

page 89 Henry Vandyke Carter/Wikimedia Commons

page 91 © Sammy Yuen

page 94 Courtesy of Bristol BioEnergy Centre, BRL, University of the West of England, Bristol, UK

page 95 Courtesy of Bristol BioEnergy Centre, BRL, University of the West of England, Bristol, UK

page 96 Turbotorque/Wikimedia Commons

page 99 Used with permission from Mayo Foundation for Medical Education and research. All Rights Reserved.

page 100 clemson/Flickr

page 103 PublicDomainPictures/Pixabay

page 104 Xavier Nájera/Wikimedia Commons

page 106 Ajzh2074/Wikimedia Commons

page 107 Brien Aho/U.S. Navy

page 108 Futurilla/Flickr

page 112 Christoph Bock (Max Planck Institute for Informatics)/Wikimedia Commons

page 113 © Hakat/iStockphoto

page 116 (rats) © Jagodka/Shutterstock; (Pope Innocent VIII) Marque Louis-Philippe/Wikimedia Commons

page 117 Mass Communication Specialist 2nd Class Daniel Gay/U.S. Navy

page 119 422737/Pixabay (no attribution required)

page 120 © AP Photo

page 121 (scan) Xavier Gigandet et. al./Wikimedia Commons; (stimoceiver) © gecko753/iStockphoto

INDEX

Page numbers in *italics* refer to illustrations.

domesticated, 44
domestic dogs, 44, 47
Downey, Tom, 91
dragon. *See* olm

East Africa, 43–44
endangered animals, 68
endangered plants, 37, 40
esophagus, 62
extinction, 58
eyesight
    correction surgery, *106*, 106–9, *107*, 134
    x-ray vision, 106–9, 134

Fairchild, Lydia, 103
Fawcett, Percy, 75, *75*, 77
fecal transplant, 86–88
Fishlake National Forest, 6
fleeceflower roots, *2*, 2–5, *3*, *4*, 127
flies, 18
flowers
    color and scent, 13
    corpse flower, 15–19, *16*, *17*
    flower power, 33–37, *34*, *35*, *36*, 129
    western moonflower, 34–36, 129
forests, 6
Frankenstein's fix, 89–92, 133
Fruita, Colorado, 60, 63
fungi, 1
    Ophiocordyceps, *24*, 24–27, *25*
    parasitic, 24
    plants compared to, 27
    trees and network of, 13
    wood-wide web or fungus network, 13

gastrointestinal, 87
gene therapy, 111, 113, 135
genetics, 111
Ghana, West Africa, 38, *38*

parasitic, 24

Patella vulgata (common European limpet), *51*, 51–55, *52*

pee power, 93–97

permafrost, 23

Pinedo, Jorge, 76

plants, 1. *See also specific topics*
    activity on uses of, 32
    animal defense of, 13–14
    chemical defense signals of, 13
    communication, 11–13
    communication with seeds, 12
    endangered, 37, 40
    fact or fake, 5, 128
    fungi compared to, 27
    identification activity, 12
    learning, 11
    protecting, 40
    real names activity, 23, 129
    secret lives of, 10–14
    sensing and reacting, 10
    talking about, 19

pollination, 13, 18
    cross-pollination, 36

poop, 85–88, *88*

Postojna, 64, 68

Praya dubia (siphonophores), 79–83, *80, 81, 82*

Proteus anguinus (olm), *64*, 64–68, *65, 66*

protozoa, 86

pseudoscorpions, *47, 48*, 48–50

public health policy, individual rights and, 96

quaking aspen groves, 8

radula, 51, 52

raptor, *71*, 71–73, *72*, 132

remote control
    of brain, 119–22
    TV remote, 119, *119*

remotely operated vehicles (ROVs), 80

researchers, professional, 123

Roosegaarde, Daan, 36, 129
root bridges, 29–32, *30*, *31*
roots
    medicinal, 2
    royal fleeceflower, 2, 2–5, *3*, *4*, 127
ROVs. *See* remotely operated vehicles
royal fleeceflower root, 2, 2–5, *3*, *4*, 127
Ryan, Jeanne, 113, 114, 135

SAD. *See* sudden aspen decline
salamander, cave-dwelling, *64*, 64–68, *65*, *66*
Santharia, 20, 23, 128
sea creatures, 54, 83, 130
search engines, 123–24
seeds, 12, *12*
shyness, cure for, 110–14, 135
siphonophores (*Praya dubia*), 79–83, *80*, *81*, *82*
Slovenia, 64, 67–68
slyrking (walking moss), 20–23, *21*, *22*, *128*
sociability, genetics and, 111
Sohan, Pakih, 30
sources
    checking for reliable, 123–26
    internet, 123–25
    interviews, 126
    library, 125
    personal logic and, 126
spider silk, 53
spores, 24, 25
Standford, Bradley, 108–9
Sternfield, Charlotte, 111, 112
stimoceiver, 120
stool, 87–88, *88*. *See also* poop
stool banks, 87–88
sudden aspen decline (SAD), 8–9
sugar, 38, 40
Sumatra, 15, 18, 29
superorganisms, 79, 83
superpowers, 106, 109

surgery. *See also* transplants
    eyesight correction, *106*, 106–9, *107*, 134
    neurosurgeon, 90
    strange, 88, 134
suspension bridge, 29, *29*
Svalbard, 20, *20*, 22, 128
symbiotic, 46, 47
Synsepalum dulcificum (agbayun), *38*, 38–41, *39*

toxin, 11, 13
transfusion, 116, 117, 118
transplants
    fecal, 86–88
    head, 89–92, *91*, 133
    kidney, 104–5
trash bugs (lacewing larvae), 128
tree octopods, 56–59, *57*, *58*, 131
trees
    acacia tree, 11, *11*
    banyan tree, 30
    fungus network and, 13
    Pando, *6*, 6–9, *7*, *8*
tuber fleeceflower, 2
TV remote control, 119, *119*
twins, 102–3
Two Medicine Formation, 70

Umshiang Double Decker Root Bridge, *31*, 31–32
University of the West of England, 93
University of Washington, 121
urine, 93–97
USDA's Animal and Plant Health Inspection Service, 5

Valles Padilla, Jose, 76
Venus flytrap, 10, *10*
vine bridges, *28*, 28–29, *29*

walking moss (slyrking), 20–23, *21*, *22*
wallflower, cure for, 110–14, 135

Warner, Greg, 76, 78
Warner, Mike, 75–78
wasps, *13*, 14
wastewater treatment plants, 96
West Africa, *38*, 38–40
western moonflower (*Ipomoea alba lucifera*), 34–36, 129
Whittaker, R. H., 27
Wikipedia, 124
wisteria plant vines, *28*, 28–29, *29*
wood-wide web (fungus network), 13

x-ray eyes, 106–9, 134

yacumama (giant anaconda), *74–75*, 74–78, *76*, *77*, 132
Yale University, 120

Zapato, Lyle, 57, 131
zombie fungus. *See Ophiocordyceps*
zombie-making fungi. *See Ophiocordyceps*